500 FACTS
Extinct

500 FACTS
Extinct

Miles Kelly

First published in 2010 by Miles Kelly Publishing Ltd
Harding's Barn, Bardfield End Green, Thaxted, Essex, CM6 3PX, UK

2 4 6 8 10 9 7 5 3 1

Editorial Director Belinda Gallagher

Art Director Jo Brewer

Cover Designer Simon Lee

Designers Sally Lace, Simon Lee, Sophie Pelham,
Andrea Slane, Tom Slemmings

Junior Designer Kayleigh Allen

Editor Sarah Parkin

Indexer Indexing Specialists (UK) Ltd

Production Manager Elizabeth Collins

Reprographics Anthony Cambray, Stephan Davis,
Jennifer Hunt, Ian Paulyn

Assets Manager Bethan Ellish

Contributors Camilla de la Bedoyere, Dr Jim Flegg,
Rupert Matthews, Steve Parker

ISBN 978-1-84810-311-5

Printed in China

British Library Cataloguing-in-Publication Data
A catalogue record for this book is available from the British Library

Made with paper from a sustainable forest

www.mileskelly.net
info@mileskelly.net

www.factsforprojects.com

Self-publish your
children's book

buddingpress.co.uk

Contents

ACKNOWLEDGEMENTS 224

Recreating the past

1 Without fossils, we would know nothing about prehistoric life. Fossils are the remains of animals and plants that died a very long time ago and became preserved in rocks. These remains are our 'window on the past'. They show us the amazing variety of life that thrived and then disappeared over millions of years of Earth's history.

▲ A preserved rhinoceros skeleton gradually emerges from ten-million-year-old rocks at a fossil excavation or 'dig' in Nebraska, USA. Removing the remains is just the first part of recreating how this great beast looked, lived and died.

What are fossils?

2 Fossils are the preserved remains of once-living things, such as bones, teeth and claws. Usually the remains were buried in sediments – layers of tiny particles such as sand, silt or mud. Very slowly, the layers and the remains inside them turned into solid rock.

3 In general it takes at least 10,000 years, but usually millions, for fossils to form. So the remains of living things that are a few hundred or thousand years old, such as the bandage-wrapped mummies of pharaohs in ancient Egypt, are not true fossils.

▲ A seed cone fossil of the extinct plant *Williamsonia*.

4 Many kinds of once-living things have formed fossils. They include all kinds of animals from enormous whales and dinosaurs to tiny flies and beetles. There are fossils of plants too, from small mosses and flowers to immense trees. Even microscopic bacteria have been preserved.

◀ Teeth are very hard and so make excellent fossils – especially those from *Tyrannosaurus rex*!

▶ It is unusual for thin, delicate bones, such as those of the bat *Icaronycteris*, to fossilize.

5 In most cases, fossils formed from the hard parts of living things that did not rot away soon after death. As well as bones, teeth and claws these include shells, scales and the bark, roots, cones and seeds of plants.

6 Much more rarely, soft parts have been preserved as fossils, such as flower petals and worm bodies. Where this has happened, it gives a fascinating glimpse into how these ancient life-forms looked and lived.

▼ The tube worms' soft bodies soon decayed but their hard, coiled tubes were preserved in the seabed mud.

Fossils in myth and legend

7 Centuries ago, the word 'fossil' was used for anything dug out of the ground. This included strange-shaped rocks, crystals and gold nuggets. However 'fossil' gradually came to mean the remains of once-living plants or animals.

▲ Fossilized *Gryphea* oyster shells were known as 'devil's toenails' due to their curved shape.

8 Long ago, some people regarded fossils as rocks and stones that had been specially shaped by gods to resemble animal teeth, tree bark and similar items. People believed this could be to show the gods' great powers and to test the faith of believers.

▶ It was once believed that ammonites (prehistoric sea creatures) were snakes that had turned to stone. This ammonite fossil has had a snake's head carved on it.

I DON'T BELIEVE IT!

The ancient Greeks likened ammonite fossils to coiled goat horns, believing them to be sacred because they associated them with the horned god, Jupiter Ammon.

9 In some parts of the world, fossils were seen as the remains of animals that perished in a terrible catastrophe. An example was the Great Flood as described in the Bible. A man named Noah managed to save many creatures by building an ark, but most perished in the rising waters.

◀ Bird or dinosaur? This small dinosaur was preserved with its body covering of feathers.

10 In ancient China, people once regarded fossils as the remains of dragons, giant serpents and similar monsters. Modern science shows that such animals never existed, but they seemed very real to people many years ago because they featured in tales of myth and legend.

11 Some fossils had their own myths. Rod-like fossils with pointed ends come from inside the bodies of belemnites, which were prehistoric relatives of squid. They were called 'thunderstones' from the belief that they formed when lightning hit the ground.

▶ Belemnites were ancient sea creatures related to cuttlefish and octopuses. The fossilized pointed shell from inside the body is sometimes called a 'belemnite bullet'.

13

Fossils get scientific

12 **People turned to science to explain fossils.** Danish geologist (rock expert) Nicolas Steno (1638–1686) noticed that objects called 'tongue stones' looked similar to the teeth of living sharks. He wondered if the teeth of ancient sharks had turned to stone.

▶ Nicolas Steno made sketches of the strange, pointed 'rocks' he found, and saw that they were similar in shape to the teeth of living sharks.

13 **French scientist Georges Cuvier (1769–1832) showed that fossils of elephants were similar to those living today.** He suggested they had become extinct – died out forever. This caused a great stir. Most people at that time believed God created animals and plants and would never let any of them die out.

▶ Cuvier recognized several extinct elephants including the woolly mammoth (right).

I DON'T BELIEVE IT!

Before scientists could explain how fossils formed, bones of huge animals such as dinosaurs were thought to be from human giants — some more than 5 metres tall!

14 In the 1820s, English doctor Gideon Mantell (1790–1852) found some huge fossil teeth similar to those of the iguana lizard, but bigger. He called the beast they came from *Iguanodon*. This was the first dinosaur to be named. Soon the search was on for fossils of more dinosaurs and other extinct animals.

15 In 1859, English naturalist Charles Darwin (1809–1882) published his book *On The Origin of Species*. In it, Darwin suggested that species (kinds) of living things that could not succeed in the struggle for survival died out or changed into new kinds, leaving fossils on the way.

16 During the 1800s, palaeontology became a new and important branch of science. This is the study of prehistoric life and it relies greatly on fossils of all kinds.

◄ Darwin examined fossils of the giant sloth *Megatherium* and wrote: "Existing animals have a close relation in form to extinct species."

How fossils form

▼ All living things die. Those living in water, such as this ichthyosaur, are more likely to leave fossils than those on land.

17 When a living thing dies, its flesh and other soft parts start to rot. Sometimes they are eaten by scavenging creatures such as worms and insects. The harder parts, such as teeth and bones, rot more slowly and last longer.

18 Fossil formation usually begins like this, and very often in water. Sediments tend to settle on dead animals and plants in ponds, lakes, rivers and seas. This is the main reason why most fossils are of plants and animals that lived in water or somehow got washed into water.

1. After death, the ichthyosaur sinks to the seabed. Worms, crabs and other scavengers eat its soft body parts.

START SOME FOSSILS

You will need:
small stones   glass mixing jug
sand   water
Imagine the stones are 'bones' of an ancient creature. They get washed into a river – put them in the jug and half-fill with water. Then the 'bones' are covered by sediment – sprinkle in the sand.

20 Water trickles into the sediments and once-living remains. The water contains dissolved substances such as minerals and salts. Gradually, these replace the once-living parts and turn them and the sediments into solid rock. This is called permineralization.

21 Most living things rot away soon after death, so the chances of anything becoming a fossil are slim. Also, sedimentary rock layers change over time, becoming heated and bent, which can destroy fossils in them. The chances of anyone finding a fossil are even tinier. This is why the record of fossils in rocks represents only a tiny proportion of prehistoric life.

19 Over time, more sediment layers settle on top of the remains. As they are covered deeper, further rotting or scavenging is less likely.

2. Sediments cover the hard body parts, such as bones and teeth, which gradually turn into solid rock.

3. Millions of years later the upper rock layers wear away and the fossil remains are exposed.

Mould and cast fossils

22 Because of the way fossils form, they are almost always found in sedimentary rocks such as sandstone, limestone, chalk, shale and slate. Other kinds of rocks, such as igneous rocks that cool from red-hot, runny lava erupted from volcanoes, do not contain fossils.

▼ Ammonites were fierce hunting animals related to squid. They died out with the dinosaurs 65 million years ago.

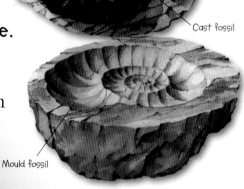

Cast fossil

Mould fossil

▲ This ammonite fossil has split into part and counterpart, with a mould and cast fossil inside.

23 As the bits and pieces of sediments become solid rock, the once-living remains within them may not. They are dissolved by water and gradually washed away. The result is a hole in the rock the same shape as the remains, called a mould fossil.

24 After more time, the hole or mould in the rock may fill with minerals deposited by water. This produces a lump of stone that is different in make-up from the surrounding rocks, but is the same shape as the original remains. This is known as a cast fossil.

25 Moulds and casts form with a whole fossil, and also with holes and spaces within a fossil. For example, the fossil skull of an animal may have a space inside where the brain once was. If this fills with minerals it can form a lump of rock that is the same size and shape as the original brain. These types of cast fossils are known as endocasts.

26 Usually, the slower fossilization happens, the more details it preserves of the original living parts. Incredible tiny features are shown even under the microscope.

▲ Sometimes many animals are fossilized together. Perhaps these fish were trapped when the water they were in dried up. Their remains show amazing detail.

I DON'T BELIEVE IT!

Fossil skulls of the ancient humans called Neanderthals show that many of them had bigger brains than people of today!

Special preservation

▲ This frog dried out before its flesh could rot away, leaving its mummified remains.

27 Once-living things can be preserved in many different ways. Mummification is when a dead plant or animal is left to dry out slowly. Some dinosaurs and animals have been preserved in this way in the windblown sands of deserts.

28 Amber is the sap (sticky resin) from prehistoric trees, especially conifers, that has been fossilized. If small creatures became trapped by the resin, they are preserved within it. Insects, spiders, frogs, and even leaves and seeds have all been preserved in this way.

◀ Amber preserves amazingly small details, even the delicate wings of this fly.

29 Natural pools of thick, sticky tar ooze up from the ground in some places such as forests and scrubland. Animals that become trapped sink into the tar pit and may be preserved – even huge creatures such as wolves, deer, bears, sabretooth cats and mammoths.

▶ In 1977, the perfectly preserved body of this baby mammoth was found thawing out in Siberia. The mammoth had been trapped in ice for thousands of years.

30 Being naturally frozen into the ice of the far north or south is a type of preservation. It's not true fossilization, but as the ice melts it reveals deep-frozen flowers, trees, mammoths and deer.

◀ Fossilized human footprints in southeastern Australia. The spacing of fossil footprints, called trackways, show how their makers walked and ran.

MATCH-UP!

Match the following with how they were preserved.
A. Desert-living dinosaur
B. Wolf in woodland
C. Tree-dwelling insect

1 Natural tar pit
2 Trapped in amber
3 Mummification.

Answers:
A3 B1 C2

31 Trace fossils are not actual body parts of once-living things. They are signs or 'traces' made by them, which then became fossilized. Examples include the footprints of animals, their burrows, egg shells, teeth marks and scratch marks, which can all turn to stone.

Fossils from jelly

32 Some rare and exciting fossils were not formed from the hard parts of living things. They were once soft creatures such as worms, jellyfish and anemones, preserved in unusual conditions.

33 Almost all living things need oxygen to survive. In some kinds of seabed mud, the water is still and brings no oxygen, so there is no life. If sea animals and plants end up here, maybe after an underwater mudslide, there are no living things to rot them in the usual way.

34 In oxygen-less conditions, dead, soft-bodied creatures and plants gradually undergo a strange type of fossilization into carbon films and impressions. These are like smears of oil or powder in the rock. They occur especially in sedimentary rocks called shales or mudstones.

◄ Jellyfish are soft and floppy, but they have on rare occasions left fossilized impressions in sand and mud.

◀ This fossil, called *Mawsonites*, may have been a jellyfish, the root-like holdfast of a seaweed or an animal's burrow network in the mud.

35 About 505 million years ago some seabed mud slid and slumped into deep, oxygen–free water. The black shale rocks that formed are at Burgess Pass in the Rocky Mountains of British Columbia, Canada.

36 Burgess Shale fossils number many tens of thousands. They include the strangest kinds of creatures resembling worms, jellyfish and shrimps. Some are like no other animals ever known.

▼ The Burgess Shale area is a World Heritage Site. It has yielded more than 60,000 fossils from the Cambrian Period, 582–488 million years ago.

37 Rare fossils give a tiny glimpse into the myriad of creatures that thrived long ago, but are rarely preserved. They show that of all the kinds of animals and plants that have ever lived, more than 999 out of 1000 are long gone and extinct (died out).

Fossils and time

38 **Fossils are studied by many kinds of scientists.** Palaeontologists are general experts on fossils and prehistoric life. Palaeozoologists specialize in prehistoric creatures, and palaeobotanists in prehistoric plants. Geologists study rocks, soil and other substances that make up the Earth. All of these sciences allow us to work out the immense prehistory of the Earth.

39 Earth's existence is divided into enormous lengths of time called eons, which are split into eras, then periods, epochs and finally, stages. Each of these time divisions is marked by changes in the rocks formed at the time – and if the rocks are sedimentary, by the fossils they contain. The whole time span, from the formation of the Earth 4600 million years ago to today, is known as the geological time scale.

▼ Starting with the Cambrian Period (far right), this timeline shows 11 major time periods in Earth's history. It gives examples of some of the fossil animals and plants that have been found for each period. 'MYA' stands for 'millions of years ago'.

NEOGENE PERIOD 23–0 MYA

Woolly mammoth
a type of
elephant

Hyracotherium
an early horse

PALEOGENE PERIOD 65–23 MYA

Parasaurolophus
a duckbilled dinosaur

CRETACEOUS PERIOD 145–65 MYA

CAMBRIAN PERIOD
542–488 MYA

Trilobite
a shelled marine creature

ORDOVICIAN PERIOD
488–444 MYA

SILURIAN PERIOD 444–416 MYA

40 An example of a geological time division is the Cretaceous Period, from 145 to 65 million years ago. It is named after creta or *kreta*, a Latin word for chalk. Due to temperature, rainfall and other climate conditions, layers of chalk rocks formed. They contained fossils such as certain kinds of shellfish, the winged reptiles known as pterosaurs and many kinds of dinosaurs.

Graptolite
a simple marine animal

Birkenia
a type of fish

Crinoid
a simple marine animal

DEVONIAN PERIOD 416–359 MYA

CARBONIFEROUS PERIOD 359–299 MYA

PERMIAN PERIOD 299–251 MYA

Lepidodendron
a primitive tree

TRIASSIC PERIOD 251–200 MYA

Diplocaulus
an early amphibian

JURASSIC PERIOD 200–145 MYA

Rhamphorhynchus
a winged reptile

Stephanoceras
a type of ammonite

MAKE CHALK FOSSILS

You will need:
chalk sticks   metal teaspoon

Chalk often contains fossil shellfish. Find pictures of long, thin examples, such as razorshells, mussels and belemnites. Use the spoon to scrape and carve the chalk sticks into shapes to make your own 'fossil' museum.

Working out dates

41 **'Dating' a fossil means finding out how old it is.** Usually, rocks found deeper in the ground are older than the rock layers above them, so any fossils they contain are also older. Sedimentary rock layers and their fossils have been compared to build up a picture of which fossilized plants and animals lived when.

▼ Different rock layers can be clearly seen in the Grand Canyon, USA. The layers have been revealed by the Colorado River as it winds its way through the canyon.

42 **If a new fossil is found, it can be compared with this overall pattern to get an idea of its age.** This is known as relative dating – finding the date of a fossil relative to other fossils of known ages.

▲ Some types of chalk rocks are almost entirely made of the fossils of small sea creatures.

43 Certain types of plants and animals were very common, survived for millions of years and left plenty of fossil remains. This makes them extremely useful for relative dating. They are known as marker, index, indicator, guide or zone fossils.

44 Most index fossils come from the sea, where preservation is more likely than on land. They include multi-legged trilobites, curly-shelled ammonites, ball-shaped echinoids (sea urchins) and net-like graptolites. On land, tough pollen grains and spores from plants are useful index fossils.

Magnetic field

N

S

▲ Earth's magnetism has changed and even reversed over millions of years, helping to date fossils.

▶ Trilobites make good index fossils. Different kinds appeared and then died out between 530 million and about 250 million years ago.

45 Earth's natural magnetic field changed many times through prehistory. When some kinds of igneous rocks formed by cooling, the magnetism was 'frozen' into them, known as palaeomagnetism. It can be dated by comparison with the whole pattern of magnetic changes through Earth's history.

How many years ago?

46 **Relative dating, by comparing fossils with each other, shows if one fossil is older or younger than another.** But how do we know the actual age of fossils in millions of years, known as absolute dating?

47 **The main kind of absolute dating is based on naturally occurring substances that give off tiny amounts of rays and particles, known as radioactivity.** As they give off these weak forms of energy, the substances – known as radioisotopes – change or 'decay' slightly. The amounts of different radioisotopes in a fossil can be measured to show how long ago it formed. This is known as radiometric dating.

48 **Several kinds of substances are used for radiometric dating.** Each decays at a set rate, some slower than others. Very slow ones are useful for the oldest fossils, and the fastest ones for young fossils.

◄ The rocks of the Canadian Shield, a huge area of land in eastern and central Canada, have been dated to more than 2500 million years ago.

49 Radiocarbon dating is based on the change or decay of one form of carbon known as C14. It happens relatively fast and is useful for a time span up to 60,000 years ago. This helps with dating young fossils and with items such as deep-frozen mammoths.

50 In potassium–argon dating, the element potassium changes into argon very slowly, over billions of years. It's useful for rock layers formed just above or below fossils from billions of years ago to about 100,000 years ago. Rubidium-strontium and uranium-lead dating can reveal the age of even older rocks, almost back to when Earth began.

▼ Geologists measure tiny amounts of radioactivity in rocks and fossils using equipment such as Geiger counters.

▼ Radiocarbon dating.

1. Woolly mammoth eats plants containing C14

2. Mammoth dies, no more C14 is taken in

3. Half of C14 decays every 5730 years

Fossil-hunting takes off

51 From the early 19th century, fossil-hunting became more popular. Towns and cities as well as rich individuals began to establish museums and collections of the 'wonders of nature' with displays of stuffed animals, pinned insects, pressed flowers – and lots of fossils.

FOSSIL MATCH

Match the scientific names of these fossils with the places they were found.

A. Argentinosaurus (dinosaur)
B. Toxorhynchites mexicanus (mosquito in amber)
C. Proconsul africanus (ape-monkey)

1 Mexico, Central America
2 Argentina, South America
3 Africa

Answers:
A2 B1 C3

52 People began to earn a living by finding and selling fossils. One of the first was Mary Anning (1799–1847) of Lyme Regis, southern England. For many years she collected fossils from the seashore, where waves and storms regularly cracked open boulders and cliffs to reveal new finds. Mary discovered fossil fish, ichthyosaurs, plesiosaurs, pterosaurs and many other animals.

▶ As in Mary Anning's time, fossils still appear from the rocks at Lyme Regis.

53 In 1881, the British Museum opened its display of natural history collections in London, which showed fossils and similar wonders from around the world. Other great cities had similar museums and sent fossil-hunters to remote places for the most spectacular finds.

▲ By the 1860s many museums had fossils on display, such as this 'sea serpent' or mosasaur.

▼ Cope and Marsh found and described about 130 new kinds of dinosaurs.

Othniel Charles Marsh

Edward Drinker Cope

54 Between the 1870s and 1890s, two of the leading fossil-hunters were Americans Othniel Charles Marsh and Edward Drinker Cope. Their teams tried to outdo each other to discover the most and best fossil dinosaurs, as well as other animals and plants too.

▲ The first fossil stegosaur skulls were found in the 1870s.

▶ The dinosaur *Stegosaurus* was named by Marsh in 1877.

55 From the early 1900s fossil-hunting spread to Africa and then in the 1920s to Mongolia and China. From the 1970s there were finds in South America and Australia. Today, fossil-hunters go all over the world in search of new discoveries.

Famous hot spots

56 Some places around the world have become famous for their fossils. These places are often in the news because of dinosaur remains. However dinosaur finds are only some of the thousands of fossils being unearthed and studied.

▼ This map shows some of the most famous fossil sites around the world.

57 The Midwest 'Badlands' of North America has many famous fossil sites. At Dinosaur National Monument, on the border between Colorado and Utah, USA, the rocks date to almost 150 million years ago. Apart from dinosaur remains they also yield fossils of crocodiles, turtles, frogs, shellfish and plants.

USA
Dinosaur
National
Monument

◀ Dinosaur fossils at Dinosaur National Monument. This park opened in 1915 and receives over 350,000 visitors each year.

BRAZIL
Santana
Formation

58 In northeast Brazil in South America there are limestone rocks about 110–90 million years old known as the Santana Formation. Detailed fossils include pterosaurs, reptiles, frogs, insects and plants. Some fossil fish were preserved with the remains of their last meals inside their bodies.

◀ This 100-million-year-old dragonfly is one of thousands from Brazil's Santana Formation rocks.

59 Some of the best European fossils come from limestone quarries around Solnhofen, southern Germany. There are dinosaurs, pterosaurs, the earliest known bird *Archaeopteryx*, fish, insects and soft-bodied jellyfish.

▲ One of the smallest dinosaurs, *Compsognathus* has been preserved in amazing detail at Solnhofen, Germany.

ERMANY
● Solnhofen

EGYPT

Fayoum

60 Lightning Ridge is in northwest New South Wales, Australia. As well as beautiful black opal gemstones there are fossils 110 million years old of long-gone mammals, dinosaurs, pterosaurs, crocodiles, turtles, sharks, crayfish, snails, shellfish and pine cones.

AUSTRALIA

Lightning Ridge

▲ Fossils of more than 400 whales such as *Basilosaurus* are known from Egypt's Fayoum area.

61 Fayoum, south of Cairo in Egypt, is one of Africa's best fossil sites. There are remains 40–25 million years old of prehistoric mammals such as hippos, rhinos, elephants, rats, bats, monkeys and even whales.

▲ Fossils of the giant wombat *Diprotodon* have been found in Australia.

Looking for fossils

62 **Where do we find fossils?**
Fossil-hunters use many kinds of aids and clues to find the best sites. Geological maps show which kinds of rocks are found at or just under the surface. To contain fossils, these rocks need to be sedimentary, such as limestone.

63 **Fossil-hunters are careful to get permission to search a site.** The landowner, land manager and local authorities must all agree on the search methods and the ownership of any finds. This avoids problems such as trespassing, criminal damage and 'fossil-rustling' (stealing).

▶ Palaeontologists sift through rocks and common fossils for signs of important specimens at Bromacker Quarry, Germany.

▶ Year after year sun, wind, rain and ice wear away rocks and reveal fossils at Dinosaur Provincial Park, Alberta, Canada.

64 Good places to look for fossils are where rocks are regularly broken apart and worn away by waves, wind, sun, ice and other weather. This is the process of erosion. It happens at cliffs, seashores, river banks and valleys, canyons and caves. It also happens where people dig quarries, mines, road and railway cuttings and building foundations.

65 Satellite images, aerial photographs, survey trips by plane, or even just walking around show the nature of the ground. Bare rocky areas are best, rather than areas covered with soil, plants and trees.

▶ This satellite photo of East Africa's Olduvai Gorge shows one of the world's best areas for prehistoric human fossils.

66 Fossil-hunters also follow a collector's code of guidelines. These show how to cause the least damage when digging, how to stay safe and how to restore the site afterwards. Find out more about this by logging on to the following web address: http://www.discovering fossils.co.uk/fossil_hunting_guidelines.htm

At the dig

67 Some people look for fossils in their spare time and if they find one it's a bonus. At an important site, scientists such as palaeontologists organize an excavation or 'dig' that can last for many months.

I DON'T BELIEVE IT!

A fossil leg bone from a huge dinosaur, being solid rock, can weigh more than one tonne!

68 The dig area is divided into squares called a grid, usually by string or strips of wood. This is used to record the positions of the finds. As the excavation continues, the workers make notes, take photographs, draw sketches and use many other recording methods.

▼ Palaeontologists dig up fossilized mammoth remains in California, USA. The valuable specimens are wrapped in layers of sacking and plaster before being moved.

69 At first there may be lots of loose rocks, boulders or soil to remove, called overburden. Big, powerful tools might be used such as mechanical diggers, road drills (jackhammers) or even dynamite!

▲ It can take weeks to clean a large fossil such as this elephant skull and tusk.

70 As fossils are exposed, experts decide whether they are worth digging out. Gradually the excavation methods become more careful, using hammers, chisels, small picks and brushes to avoid damaging the find. It can be a lengthy, difficult task. The dig site might be a baking desert, tropical swamp or freezing mountainside.

71 Small bits of loose rock might be sieved to find tiny fossils. Soft, fragile fossils can be covered with material such as plaster or fibre-glass, which hardens into a protective jacket. This allows the fossil to be lifted out.

37

Cleaning up fossils

72 When fossils reach the workroom, which might be in a museum or university, experts decide which ones to prepare. This means cleaning away unwanted bits of rock and stone around the fossil (the matrix) without damaging the fossil itself.

73 Many kinds of tools and equipment are needed to clean or expose a fossil. They range from small hammers, chisels and drills, to engraving tools, pins and picks, sanders, files and different brushes. The preparator (person working on the fossil) stops regularly to examine the specimen and decide which part to clean next.

◄ Museum preparators work carefully to remove unwanted bits of rock and leave only the fossil.

WHAT ORDER?

List these tools and equipment in the order you would use them to find, dig up and clean a rare fossil.

A. Wooden toothpick
B. Hammer and chisel
C. Stick of dynamite
D. Soft-bristled paintbrush
E. Dentist's drill

Answer:
C B E A D

74 Microscopes are often used to show tiny details of a fossil during preparation. Usually this is a stereoscopic microscope with two eyepieces, like binoculars, mounted on a stand with the specimen beneath.

▶ It may take a year to dissolve rock with acid and expose the fossils – these are unhatched dinosaur eggs.

Dinosaur embryo

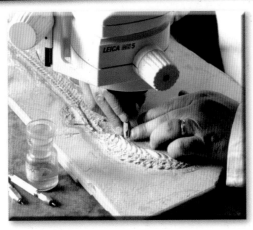

▲ The enlarged view through a stereo microscope shows lots of detail, to avoid scratching or chipping the specimen.

75 When the fossil is one type of rock and the matrix is another, preparators may use chemicals to expose the fossil. Different acids are tested on small parts of the matrix and fossil, to see if they dissolve the former but not the latter.

76 Very few animals or plants die neatly in one piece and are preserved whole. So it's incredibly rare to find a whole fossilized plant or animal with all the parts positioned as they were in life. Most fossils are bits and pieces that are crushed and distorted. Putting them back together is very difficult!

39

On display

77 In a well-organized fossil collection, specimens are given catalogue numbers showing where and when they were found. They are studied, described and identified, and logged into a computer database or card index. Then the specimen can be easily recognized.

▼ London's Natural History Museum has some of the world's best fossil displays, such as these dinosaurs.

78 Usually only exceptional fossils are chosen to display in museums, galleries and exhibitions. They might be very large for their kind, preserved in great detail, be extremely rare, found by a famous fossil-hunter, or simply very beautiful.

79 Fossil displays vary hugely. Some are shelves or cabinets with simple labels. Others have fossils and reconstructions of the original animals or plants, set into a realistic scene. They may have special lighting, descriptions and diagrams, and even press-button video shows.

I DON'T BELIEVE IT!

In 2002, experts re-examined the fossil jaws of a tiny creature called *Rhyniognatha* found in 1919. They realized it was probably the earliest known insect, and that it was almost 400 million years old.

80 **Some fossils are so rare, delicate or valuable that they are not displayed — copies are.** Copies or replicas of very rare fossils might be sent to other museums so more people can study them.

81 **Copies are used for big creatures such as dinosaurs, whales and mammoths.** The original fossils are solid rock and can weigh many tonnes. Lightweight copies are easier and safer to put on a frame or hang by wires, to build up the animal in a lifelike position.

Fossils come alive!

82 One of the most exciting parts of fossil study is to reconstruct (rebuild) the original plant or animal. This needs a detailed knowledge of anatomy, or body structure. For example, fossils of prehistoric birds are compared to the same body parts of similar birds alive today. This is called comparative anatomy.

83 Tiny marks or 'scars' on fossil bones show where the animal's muscles attached in real life. These help to reveal muscle shapes and arrangements so experts can gradually put the flesh on the (fossil) bones.

Fossil bones
Faint scars on fossil bones can help scientists work out how and where muscles were attached

▲ This reconstruction of an ankylosaur, an armoured dinosaur, is being done head–first. The tail is still bare fossils of the bones.

84 We can see how a living creature walks, runs and jumps using the joints between its bones. If fossil bones have their joints preserved, their detailed shapes and designs show the range of motion and how the animal moved.

MULTI-COLOURED BIRD

You will need:
pictures of *Archaeopteryx*   colour pens
tracing paper   white paper

No one knows what colour the first bird *Archaeopteryx* was. Look at pictures of it in books and on web sites. See how its feather colours and patterns differ. Trace an outline of *Archaeopteryx* from a book and colour it to your own amazing design.

Soft tissues
Flesh, guts and muscles can be added
to the skeleton as scientists compare
the fossil to similar living animals

Skin
The external covering of skin,
scales, horns and claws are added
by studying fossil examples and
using intelligent guess work

85 Gradually, soft parts such
as the guts of an animal or the
petals of a flower, can be guessed
and added to the reconstruction.
Again, experts use information from
fossil relatives and living cousins.

86 The outward appearance of an
animal might be known from fossils such
as an outer shell, scaly skin, feathers or
fur. However fossils are not original living
parts – they have changed to rock. So the
colour of fossil skin is the colour of the type
of rock, not the animal. Experts guess at
colours and patterns for their reconstructions.

Trading, stealing, faking

87 Fossils are big business. Thousands of people work at digs, in workrooms and in museums, exhibitions and galleries. A find such as a new dinosaur can hit the news headlines and make the discoverer famous — and rich!

88 The biggest, most complete fossil *Tyrannosaurus rex* was found in 1990 near Faith, Dakota, by Sue Hendrickson. The dinosaur was nicknamed 'Sue' and there was a long legal dispute about who owned it. Finally it was sold to the Field Museum of Chicago for more than seven million dollars!

◀ Street traders offer fossils for sale in North Africa. There is no guarantee the fossils came from the local area.

I DON'T BELIEVE IT!

I DON'T BELIEVE IT!

In 2008, a 7-metre-long fossil *Triceratops* dinosaur went on sale for £400,000 along with a fossil skull of a sabre-tooth cat for £35,000.

▶ Chinese palaeontologist Dong Zhiming with some smuggled dinosaur eggs. Every year police, customs and security staff uncover illegal collections such as this.

89 Real fossils, replicas and models are sold around the world by museums, shops, mail-order catalogues and on the Internet. Buyers range from leading museums to individuals who like the idea of a home fossil collection without the trouble of digging them up.

▼ Rare or unusual fossils, such as this ammonite shell showing detailed internal structure, can fetch huge sums of money at auction.

90 Stealing and faking fossils has been going on for centuries. In 1999 scientists announced a fossil creature called *Archaeoraptor* that seemed to be part-bird and part-dinosaur. *Archaeoraptor* showed how small meat-eating dinosaurs evolved into birds. However further study revealed that the specimen was indeed part-dinosaur and part-bird, because it was a fake with separate fossils cleverly glued together.

Famous fossils

91 Many fossils and prehistoric sites around the world are massive attractions, visited by millions of people. The Petrified Forest National Park in Arizona, USA has hundreds of huge fossilized trees and smaller specimens of animals such as dinosaurs, dating from about 225 million years ago. It receives more than half a million visitors yearly.

▲ The coelacanth is known as a 'living fossil', meaning it is very similar to its long-extinct relatives.

92 The coelacanth fish was known only from fossils and thought to have been extinct for more than 60 million years. In 1938 a living coelacanth was caught off southeast Africa and more have been discovered since. Living things that are very similar to their prehistoric relatives are known as 'living fossils'.

▶ Thousands of fossil tree trunks and branches litter the ground at Arizona's Petrified Forest National Park.

93 There are only about ten fossils of *Archaeopteryx*, the first known bird. They all come from the Solnhofen area of southern Germany. They are amazingly detailed and almost priceless.

▶ Each specimen of *Archaeopteryx* is closely guarded.

94 'Lucy' is a fossilized part-skeleton from a very early human-type creature. It was discovered in 1974 in Ethiopia, Africa and dates back about 3.2 million years. Thousands of people flock to see 'her' every year.

◀ Piltdown Man was really the skull of a human from about 500 years ago combined with the jawbone of an orang-utan.

I DON'T BELIEVE IT!

Animal droppings can become fossils known as coprolites. Leftovers in them can show what an animal ate. Luckily they are no longer squishy and smelly, but have become solid rock.

95 Piltdown Man is perhaps the most famous fossil fake. It was found in southeast England in 1912 and thought to be an early kind of human. In 1953 it was exposed as a hoax by new scientific methods.

Looking to the future

96 As fossil-hunting goes on around the world, scientific methods and equipment become more powerful every year. Ground-penetrating radar, X-rays and CT (computerized tomography) scanners can 'see' fossils inside solid rock.

▲ A CT scanner examines the fossil skull of an ancient type of otter.

97 As we improve ways to study fossils, old specimens are looked at again to see new details. The dinosaur *Oviraptor* or 'egg thief' was named because one of its fossils suggested it was stealing the eggs of another dinosaur. Then X-rays of similar eggs showed baby *Oviraptors* inside. The 'egg thief' fossil was probably looking after its own eggs.

◀ This *Oviraptor* may have died shielding its eggs from a predator, 75 million years ago.

98 Some amazing fossils of the 1990s–2000s are from Liaoning Province in northeast China. Dated to 130 million years ago, they show details of creatures and plants, including dinosaurs with feathers and a cat-sized mammal that preyed on baby dinosaurs.

▲ Fossils of the tiny feathered dinosaur *Microraptor* have been found in China.

99 New fossils provide more evidence for evolution, such as how fish changed gradually into land animals. *Panderichthys* was a fish-like creature from 380 million years ago. It had features such as finger-like bones developing in its fins.

100 Important fossil discoveries cause news and excitement around the world. They affect our ideas about prehistoric life, how Earth has changed through time, evolution and extinction. They can also help to fill in the details of where we came from.

NAME GAME

Match these nicknames of fossils with their scientific names.
A. 'Lucy' B. 'Stan' C. 'Jaws'
D. 'Spike'
1. Triceratops (dinosaur)
2. Megalodon (giant shark)
3. Australopithecus afarensis (early human)
4. Tyrannosaurus (dinosaur)

Answers:
A3 B4 C2 D1

▲ *Panderichthys* was about one metre long. Its fossils come from Latvia in northeastern Europe.

World of the dinosaurs

101 Dinosaurs were types of animals
with scaly skin, called reptiles. They lived
millions of years ago. There were many
different kinds of dinosaurs – huge and tiny,
tall and short, fierce hunters and peaceful
plant-eaters. But all the dinosaurs
died out long, long ago.

Age of the dinosaurs

102 Dinosaurs lived between about 230 million and 65 million years ago. This vast length of time is called the Mesozoic Era. Dinosaurs were around for about 80 times longer than people have been on Earth!

103 Dinosaurs were not the only animals during the Mesozoic Era. There were many other kinds of animals such as insects, fish, lizards, crocodiles, birds and mammals.

104 There were many different shapes and sizes of dinosaurs. Some were smaller than your hand. Others were bigger than a house!

▼ Jobaria and Janenschia, giant plant eaters.

▼ This timeline begins 286 million years ago at the start of the Permian Period when the ancestors of the dinosaurs appear. It finishes at the end of the Tertiary Period 2 million years ago, when the dinosaurs die out and mammals became dominant.

PALAEOZOIC ERA	MESOZOIC ERA	
PERMIAN PERIOD	TRIASSIC PERIOD	JURASSIC PERIOD
The reptiles, including the ancestors of the dinosaurs, start to become more important than the amphibians.	The first proper dinosaurs appear. These are small two-legged carnivores, meat-eaters, and larger herbivores, or plant eaters.	Many different dinosaurs lived at this time, including the giant plant eaters like Barosaurus.

Erythrosuchus

Thrinaxodon

Riojasaurus

Plateosaurus

Barosaurus

Heterodontosaurus

Apatosaurus

MILLIONS OF YEARS AGO

299   251   200   145

105
No single kind of dinosaur survived for all of the Mesozoic Era. Different dinosurs came and went. Some lasted for less than a million years. Other kinds, like Stegosaurus, kept going for more than 20 million years.

106
There were no people during the Age of Dinosaurs. There was a gap of more than 60 million years between the last dinosaurs and the first people.

I DON'T BELIEVE IT!

The name 'dinosaur' means 'terrible lizard'. But dinosaurs weren't lizards, and not all dinosaurs were terrible. Small plant-eating dinosaurs were about as 'terrible' as today's sheep!

◄ All the dinosaurs died out at the end of the Cretaceous Period, possibly because of a meteor strike, but no one can be sure.

MESOZOIC ERA	CENOZOIC ERA
CRETACEOUS PERIOD	TERTIARY PERIOD
During the last part of the age of the dinosaurs, both giant carnivores and armoured herbivores were alive.	The dinosaurs have all died out. Mammals, which have been around since the Triassic Period, become the main land animals.

Tyrannosaurus rex

Deinonychus

Spinosaurus

Tarbosaurus

Brontotherium, herbivorous mammal

Thylacosmilus, carnivorous mammal

Nesodon, herbivorous mammal

145

66

2

MILLIONS OF YEARS AGO

Before the dinosaurs

107 Dinosaurs were not the first animals on Earth. Many other kinds of creatures lived before them, including several other types of reptiles. Over millions of years one of these groups of reptiles probably changed very slowly, or evolved, into the first dinosaurs.

109 Crocodiles were around even before the first dinosaurs. They still survive today, long after the last dinosaurs. *Erythrosuchus* was 4.5 metres long, lived 240 million years ago, lurked in swamps and ate fish.

108 *Dimetrodon* was a fierce, meat-eating reptile that looked like a dinosaur — but it wasn't. It lived 270 million years ago, long before the dinosaurs. *Dimetrodon* was 3 metres long and had a tall flap of skin like a sail on its back.

110
Therapsids lived before the dinosaurs and also alongside the early dinosaurs. They were called mammal-like reptiles because they didn't have scaly skin like most reptiles. They had furry or hairy skin like mammals.

▼ Ornithosuchus was one of the early thecodonts. It was a carnivore that walked on two legs, a cousin of the first dinosaurs. The name 'thecodont' means 'socket-toothed reptile'.

111
Thecodonts were slim, long-legged reptiles that lived just before the dinosaurs. They could rear up and run fast on their back legs. They could also leap and jump well. They probably caught small animals such as bugs and lizards to eat.

112
Of all the creatures shown here, the thecodonts were most similar to the first dinosaurs. So perhaps some thecodonts gradually changed, or evolved, into early dinosaurs. This may have happened more than 220 million years ago. But no one is sure, and there are many other ideas about where the dinosaurs came from.

The dinosaurs arrive!

113 The earliest dinosaurs stalked the Earth almost 230 million years ago. They lived in what is now Argentina, in South America. They included *Eoraptor* and *Herrerasaurus*. Slim and fast creatures, they could stand almost upright and run on their two rear legs. Few other animals of the time could run upright like this, on legs that were straight below their bodies. Most other animals had legs that stuck out sideways.

Herrerasaurus was about 3 metres long from nose to tail.

The legs were underneath the body, not sticking out to the sides as in other reptiles, such as lizards and crocodiles.

114

These early dinosaurs were probably meat eaters. They hunted small reptiles such as lizards, insects and worms. They had lightweight bodies and long, strong legs to chase after prey. Their claws were long and sharp for grabbing victims. Their large mouths were filled with pointed teeth to tear up their food.

TWO LEGS GOOD!

You will need:

some stiff card
safe scissors

sticky tape
split pins

Cut out a model of *Herrerasaurus*; the head, body, arms and tail are one piece of card. Next, cut out each leg from another piece. Fix the legs on either side of the hip area of the body using a split pin. Adjust the angle of the head, body and tail to stand over the legs. This is how many dinosaurs stood and ran, well balanced over their rear legs and using little effort.

Herrerasaurus had a pointed head and a long, bendy neck, which helped it to look around and sniff for prey.

The long tail balanced the head and body over the rear legs.

Herrerasaurus could run rapidly on its two rear legs, or walk slowly on all fours.

Getting bigger!

115 As the early dinosaurs spread over the land they began to change. This gradual and natural change in living things has happened since life began on Earth. New kinds of plants and animals appear, do well for a time, and then die out as yet more new kinds appear. The slow and gradual change of living things over time is called evolution.

Plateosaurus

116 Some kinds of dinosaurs became larger and began to eat plants rather than animals. *Plateosaurus* was one of the first big plant-eating dinosaurs. It grew up to 8 metres long and lived 220 million years ago in what is now Europe. It could rear up on its back legs and use its long neck to reach food high off the ground.

117 *Riojasaurus* was an even larger plant eater. It lived 218 million years ago in what is now Argentina. *Riojasaurus* was 10 metres long and weighed about 2 tonnes - more than a large family car of today.

Riojasaurus

118 The early dinosaurs lived during the Triassic Period. This was the first period or part of the Age of Dinosaurs (the Mesozoic Era). The Triassic Period lasted from 251 to 200 million years ago.

119 The early plant-eating dinosaurs may have become larger so that they could reach up into trees for food. Their size would also have helped them fight enemies, as many big meat-eating reptiles were ready to make a meal of them. One was the crocodile *Rutiodon* which was 3 metres long.

▼ *Rutiodon*, a crocodile-like meat eater, waits for *Riojasaurus*. It may be thinking about dinner!

I DON'T BELIEVE IT!

Early plant-eating dinosaurs did not eat fruits or grasses — there weren't any! They hadn't appeared yet! Instead they ate plants called horsetails, ferns, cycads, and conifer trees.

What teeth tell us

120 **We know about living things from long ago, such as dinosaurs, because of fossils.** These were once their hard body parts, such as bones, claws, horns and shells. The hard parts did not rot away after death but got buried and preserved for millions of years. Gradually they turned to stone and became fossils. Today, we dig up the fossils, and their sizes and shapes give us clues to how prehistoric animals lived.

▶ Plant eater *Edmontosaurus* had flat teeth at the back of its jaws for chewing its food.

121 **Dinosaur teeth were very hard and formed many fossils.** Their shapes help to show what each type of dinosaur ate. *Edmontosaurus* had rows of broad, wide, sharp-ridged teeth in the sides of its mouth. These were ideal for chewing tough plant foods like twigs and old leaves.

▲ *Tyrannosaurus rex* had sharp, knife-like teeth at the front of its jaw for cutting and tearing meat.

122 ***Tarbosaurus* had long, sharp teeth like knives or daggers.** These were excellent for tearing up victims, and slicing off lumps of flesh for swallowing.

▲ *Tarbosaurus* was 12 metres long and lived 70 million years ago in East Asia.

▼ Baryonyx was 10 metres long and lived 120 million years ago in Europe.

FIND DINOSAUR TEETH AT HOME!

With the help of an adult, look in a utensils drawer or tool box for dinosaur teeth! Some tools resemble the teeth of some dinosaurs, and do similar jobs.
File or rasp – broad surface with hard ridges, like the plant-chewing teeth of *Edmontosaurus*.
Knife – long, pointed and sharp, like the meat-slicing teeth of *Tyrannosaurus rex*.
Pliers – Gripping and squeezing, like the beak-shaped mouth of *Ornithomimus*.

123 Baryonyx had small, narrow, pointed, cone-shaped teeth. These resemble the teeth of a crocodile or dolphin today. They are ideal for grabbing slippery prey such as fish.

124 The teeth of the giant, long-necked dinosaur *Apatosaurus* were long, thin and blunt, shaped like pencils. They worked like a rake to pull leaves off branches into the mouth, for the dinosaur to eat.

▶ Apatosaurus was 25 metres long and lived 140 million years ago in Western North America.

125 Some dinosaurs, like *Ornithomimus*, had no teeth at all! The mouth was shaped like a bird's beak and made out of a tough, strong, horny substance like our fingernails. The beak was suited to pecking up all kinds of food such as seeds, worms and bugs.

▲ Ornithomimus was 3.5 metres long and lived 70 million years ago in western North America.

Super-size dinosaurs

126 The true giants of the Age of Dinosaurs were the sauropods. These vast dinosaurs all had a small head, long neck, barrel-shaped body, long tapering tail and four pillar-like legs. The biggest sauropods included *Brachiosaurus, Mamenchisaurus, Barosaurus, Diplodocus* and *Argentinosaurus.*

▲ *Argentinosaurus* was up to 40 metres long, and weighed up to 100 tonnes.

127 Sauropod dinosaurs probably lived in groups or herds. We know this from their footprints, which have been preserved as fossils. Each foot left a print as large as a chair seat. Hundreds of footprints together shows that many sauropods walked along in groups.

128 Sauropod dinosaurs may have swallowed pebbles — on purpose! Their peg-like teeth could only rake in plant food, not chew it. Pebbles and stones gulped into the stomach helped to grind and crush the food. These pebbles, smooth and polished by the grinding, have been found with the fossil bones of sauropods.

Mamenchisaurus grew up to 26 metres long and weighed 30 tonnes. It lived in East Asia 160 million years ago.

129 The biggest sauropods like *Apatosaurus* were enormous beasts. They weighed up to ten times more than elephants of today. Yet their fossil footprints showed they could run quite fast – nearly as quickly as you!

Barosaurus lived 150 million years ago in North America and Africa. It was 27 metres long and weighed 15 tonnes.

Brachiosaurus grew up to 25 metres long, and weighed up to 50 tonnes. It lived 150 million years ago in North America and Africa.

Diplodocus lived in North America 150 million years ago. It grew to 27 metres long and weighed up to 12 tonnes.

130 Sauropods probably had to eat most of the time, 20 hours out of every 24. They had enormous bodies that needed great amounts of food, but only small mouths to gather the food.

TI717 – 011

This modern lorry is to the same scale as these huge dinosaurs!

I DON'T BELIEVE IT!

Diplodocus is also known as 'Old Whip–tail'! It could swish its long tail so hard and fast that it made an enormous CRACK like a whip. This living, leathery, scaly whip would scare away enemies or even rip off their skin.

Claws for killing

131 **Nearly all dinosaurs had claws on their fingers and toes.** These claws were shaped for different jobs in different dinosaurs. They were made from a tough substance called keratin – the same as your fingernails and toenails.

132 *Hypsilophodon* **had strong, sturdy claws.** This small plant eater, 2 metres long, probably used them to scrabble and dig in soil for seeds and roots.

133 *Deinonychus* **had long, sharp, hooked claws on its hands.** This meat eater, about 3 metres long, would grab a victim and tear at its skin and flesh.

Deinonychus

134 *Deinonychus* **also had a huge hooked claw, as big as your hand, on the second toe of each foot.** This claw could kick out and flick down like a pointed knife to slash pieces out of the prey.

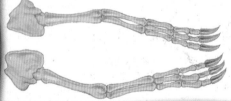

135 *Baryonyx* **also had a large claw but this was on the thumb of each hand.** It may have worked as a fish-hook to snatch fish from water. This is another clue that *Baryonyx* probably ate fish.

◄ These giant arms of the dinosaur *Deinocheirus* were found in Mongolia. Each one was bigger than a human, but nothing else of the skeleton has yet been found.

136 *Iguanodon* had claws on its **feet.** But these were rounded and blunt and looked more like hooves.

137 *Iguanodon* also had stubby **claws on its hands.** However its thumb claw was longer and shaped like a spike, perhaps for stabbing enemies.

138 Giant sauropod **dinosaurs had almost flat claws.** Dinosaurs like *Apatosaurus* looked like they had toenails on their huge feet!

Deadly meat eaters

139 The biggest meat-eating dinosaurs were the largest predators (hunters) ever to walk the Earth. Different types came and went during the Age of Dinosaurs. *Allosaurus* was from the middle of this time span. One of the last dinosaurs was also one of the largest predators – *Tyrannosaurus rex.* An earlier hunting dinosaur from South America was even bigger – *Giganotosaurus.*

140

These great predators were well equipped for hunting large prey – including other dinosaurs. They all had massive mouths armed with long sharp teeth in powerful jaws. They had long, strong back legs for fast running, and enormous toe claws for kicking and holding down victims.

141

Meat-eating dinosaurs probably caught their food in various ways. They may have lurked behind rocks or trees and rushed out to surprise a victim. They may have raced as fast as possible after prey that ran away or plodded steadily for a great time to tire out their meal. They might even have scavenged – feasted on the bodies of creatures which were dead or dying.

Albertosaurus was from North America. It was 9 metres long and weighed one tonne

Allosaurus was 11 metres long and weighed 2 tonnes. It came from North America

Spinosaurus came from Africa. It was 14 metres long and weighed 4 tonnes

Carnotaurus from South America was 7.5 metres long and weighed one tonne

The famous *Tyrannosaurus rex* was 13 metres long and weighed 5 tonnes. It lived in North America.

The biggest carnivore was *Giganotosaurus*. It was over 13 metres long and weighed over 6 tonnes

Look! Listen! Sniff!

142 **Like the reptiles of today, dinosaurs could see, hear and smell the world around them.** We know this from fossils. The preserved fossil skulls have spaces for eyes, ears and nostrils.

143 **Some dinosaurs like *Troodon* had very big eyes.** There are large, bowl-shaped hollows in their fossil skulls. Today's animals with big eyes can see well in the dark, like mice, owls and night-time lizards. Perhaps *Troodon* prowled through the forest at night, peering in the gloom for small creatures to eat.

Ear

Eye

Nostril

144 **There are also spaces on the sides of the head where *Troodon* had its ears.** Dinosaur ears were round and flat, like the ears of other reptiles. *Troodon* could hear the tiny noises of little animals moving about in the dark.

◀ *Troodon* was about 2 metres long and lived in North America 70 million years ago. You can see here the large eye sockets.

145

The nostrils of *Troodon*, where it breathed in air and smelled scents, were two holes at the front of its snout. With its delicate sense of smell, *Troodon* could sniff out its prey of insects, worms, little reptiles such as lizards, and small shrew-like mammals.

▲ *Corythosaurus* had a bony plate on its head, instead of a tube like *Parasaurolophus*.

146

Dinosaurs used their eyes, ears and noses not only to find food, but also to detect enemies — and each other. *Parasaurolophus* had a long, hollow, tube-like crest on its head. Perhaps it blew air along this to make a noise like a trumpet, as an elephant does today with its trunk.

▶ *Parasaurolophus* was a 'duck-billed' dinosaur or hadrosaur. It was about 10 metres long and lived 80 million years ago in North America.

BIGGER EYES, BETTER SIGHT

Make a *Troodon* mask from card. Carefully cut out the shape as shown. Carefully cut out two small eye holes, each just one cm across. Attach elastic so you can wear the mask and find out how little you can see. Carefully make the eye holes as large as the eyes of the real *Troodon*. Now you can have a much bigger, clearer view of the world!

147

Dinosaurs like *Parasaurolophus* may have made noises to send messages to other members of their group or herd. Different messages could tell the others about finding food or warn them about enemies.

69

Living with dinosaurs

148 **All dinosaurs walked and ran on land, as far as we know.** No dinosaurs could fly in the air or spend their lives swimming in the water. But many other creatures, which lived at the same time as the dinosaurs, could fly or swim. Some were reptiles, like the dinosaurs.

149 **Ichthyosaurs were reptiles that lived in the sea.** They were shaped like dolphins, long and slim with fins and a tail. They chased after fish to eat.

150 **Plesiosaurs were also reptiles that swam in the sea.** They had long necks, tubby bodies, four large flippers and a short tail.

151 **Turtles were another kind of reptile that swam in the sea during the Age of Dinosaurs.** Each had a strong, domed shell and four flippers. Turtles still survive today, but ichthyosaurs and plesiosaurs died out with the dinosaurs, long ago.

Turtle

Plesiosaur

Ichthyosaur

▼ Hadrosaurs like *Anatosaurus* were duck-billed dinosaurs with a long, wide tail like a crocodile's tail. Perhaps Anatosaurus swished this from side to side to swim now and again. But it did not live in the water.

◄ Predators like *Velociraptor* were meat-eating dinosaurs with large arms, wrists and hands. Over millions of years these could have evolved feathers to become a bird's wings.

153 Birds first appeared about 150 million years ago. It is possible that over millions of years certain small, meat-eating dinosaurs called raptors developed feathers. Slowly their arms became wings. Gradually they evolved into the very first birds.

154 Birds evolved after the dinosaurs, but birds did overlap with the dinosaurs. Some dived for fish in the sea, very much like birds such as gulls and terns today.

Ichthyornis

152 Pterosaurs were reptiles that could fly. They had thin, skin-like wings held out by long finger bones. Some soared over the sea and grabbed small fish in their sharp-toothed, beak-shaped mouths. Others swooped on small land animals.

Rhamphorynchus

QUIZ

Which of these are NOT dinosaurs?

A Pterosaur

B Raptor

C Plesiosaur

D Hadrosaur

E Ichthyosaur

F Bird

Answers:
A Pterosaur, C Plesiosaur,
E Ichthyosaur, F Bird

Fastest and slowest

155 **Dinosaurs walked and ran at different speeds, according to their size and shape.** In the world today, cheetahs and ostriches are slim with long legs and run very fast. Elephants and hippos are massive heavyweights and plod slowly. Dinosaurs were similar. Some were big, heavy and slow. Others were slim, light and speedy.

▼ *Coelophysis* was 3 metres long. It was one of the earliest dinosaurs, living about 220 million years ago.

▲ *Struthiomimus* lived about 75 million years ago in north-west North America.

156 **Struthiomimus was one of the fastest of all the dinosaurs.** It was more than 2 metres tall and 4 metres long. It had very long back legs and large clawed feet, like an ostrich. It also had a horny beak-shaped mouth for pecking food, like an ostrich. This is why it is also called an 'ostrich-dinosaur'. It could probably run at more than 70 kilometres per hour.

157 *Muttaburrasaurus* was a huge ornithopod type of dinosaur, a cousin of *Iguanodon*. It probably walked about as fast as you, around 4–5 kilometres per hour. It might have been able to gallop along at a top speed of 15 kilometres per hour, making the ground shake with its 4-tonne weight!

▲ *Muttaburrasaurus* lived about 110 million years ago in south-east Australia.

158 *Coelophysis* was a slim, lightweight dinosaur. It could probably trot, jump, leap and dart about with great agility. Sometimes it ran upright on its two back legs. Or it could bound along on all fours like a dog at more than 30 kilometres per hour.

QUIZ

Put these dinosaurs and today's animals in order of top running speed, from slowest to fastest.

Human (40 km/h)

Cheetah (100–plus km/h)

Struthiomimus (70 km/h)

Muttaburrasaurus (15 km/h)

Sloth (0.2 km/h)

Coelophysis (30 km/h)

Answer:
Sloth, *Muttaburrasaurus*, *Coelophysis*, Human, *Struthiomimus*, Cheetah

Dinosaur tanks

159 **Some dinosaurs had body defences against predators.** These might be large horns and spikes, or thick hard lumps of bonelike armour-plating. Most armoured dinosaurs were plant eaters. They had to defend themselves against big meat-eating dinosaurs such as *Tyrannosaurus rex*.

160 ***Triceratops* had three horns, one on its nose and two much longer ones above its eyes.** It also had a wide shield-like piece of bone over its neck and shoulders. The horns and neck frill made *Triceratops* look very fearsome. But most of the time it quietly ate plants. If it was attacked, *Triceratops* could charge at the enemy and jab with its horns, like a rhino does today.

▲ *Triceratops* was 9 metres long and weighed over 5 tonnes. It lived 65 million years ago in North America.

161 *Euoplocephalus* was a well-armoured dinosaur. It had bands of thick, leathery skin across its back. Big, hard, pointed lumps of bone were set into this skin like studs on a leather belt. *Euoplocephalus* also had a great lump of bone on its tail. It measured almost one metre across and looked like a massive hammer or club. *Euoplocephalus* could swing it at predators to injure them or break their legs.

Styracosaurus

DESIGN A DINOSAUR!

Make an imaginary dinosaur! It might have the body armour and tail club of *Euoplocephalus*, or the head horns and neck frill of *Triceratops*.
You can draw your dinosaur, or make it out of pieces of card or from modelling clay. You can give it a made-up name, like Euoplo-ceratops or Tri-cephalus.
How well protected is your dinosaur? How does it compare to some well-armoured creatures of today, such as a tortoise, armadillo or porcupine?

Protoceratops

Euoplocephalus

Dinosaur eggs and nests

162 Like most reptiles today, dinosaurs produced young by laying eggs. These hatched out into baby dinosaurs, which gradually grew into adults. Fossils have been found of eggs with developing dinosaurs inside, as well as fossils of just-hatched baby dinosaurs.

▼ A female *Protoceratops* with her eggs.

163 Many kinds of dinosaur eggs have been found. *Protoceratops* was a pig-sized dinosaur that lived 85 million years ago in what is now the Gobi Desert of Asia.

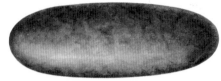

Protoceratops' egg

164 A *Protoceratops* female arranged her eggs. The eggs were carefully positioned in a spiral shape, or in circles one within the other.

165

Protoceratops scraped a bowl-shaped nest about one metre across in the dry soil. Probably the female did this. Today, only female reptiles make nests and some care for the eggs or babies. Male reptiles take no part.

Hadrosaur egg

166

The eggs probably hatched after a few weeks. The eggshell was slightly leathery and bendy, like most reptile eggshells today, and not brittle or hard like a bird's.

167

Fossils of baby Protoceratops show that they looked very much like their parents. But the neck frill of the baby Protoceratops was not as large compared to the rest of the body, as in the adult. As the youngster grew, the frill grew faster than the rest of the body.

► This shows part of a Tyrannosaurus rex egg.

QUIZ

1. How long was Triceratops?
2. How many horns did Triceratops have?
3. How many eggs did a female Protoceratops lay?
4. Did dinosaurs lay hard eggs like birds, or bendy eggs?
5. How long was a Tyrannosaurus rex egg?

Answers:
1. 9 metres 2. Three
3. About 20 eggs 4. They laid bendy,
leathery eggs 5. 40 centimetres

168

Other dinosaurs laid different sizes and shapes of eggs. Huge sauropod dinosaurs like Brachiosaurus probably laid rounded eggs as big as basketballs. Eggs of big meat-eaters like Tyrannosaurus were more sausage-shaped, 40 centimetres long and 15 centimetres wide.

169

Most dinosaurs simply laid their eggs in a nest or buried in soil, and left them to hatch on their own. The baby dinosaurs had to find their own food and defend themselves against enemies. But other dinosaurs looked after their babies.

Dinosaur babies

170 **Some dinosaur parents looked after their babies and even brought them food in the nest.** Fossils of the hadrosaur dinosaur *Maiasaura* include nests, eggs, babies after hatching, and broken eggshells. Some fossils are of unhatched eggs but broken into many small parts, as though squashed by the babies which had already come out of their eggs.

171 **The newly-hatched *Maiasaura* babies had to stay in the nest.** They could not run away because their leg bones had not yet become strong and hard. The nest was a mound of mud about 2 metres across, and up to 20 babies lived in it.

▶ Hundreds of fossil *Maiasaura* nests have been found close together, showing that these dinosaurs bred in groups or colonies. The nests show signs of being dug out and repaired year after year, which suggests the dinosaurs kept coming back to the same place to breed.

▲ A full-grown *Maiasaura* was about 9 metres long and weighed around 3 tonnes. A newly-hatched *Maiasaura* baby was only 30–40 centimetres long. *Maiasaura* lived about 75 million years ago in North America.

172 Fossils of *Maiasaura* nests also contain fossilised twigs, berries and other bits of plants. *Maiasaura* was a plant-eating dinosaur, and it seems that one or both parents brought food to the nest for their babies to eat. The tiny teeth of the babies already had slight scratches and other marks where they had been worn while eating food. This supports the idea that parent *Maiasaura* brought food to their babies in the nest.

I DON'T BELIEVE IT!

Baby dinosaurs grew up to five times faster than human babies! A baby sauropod dinosaur like *Diplodocus* was already one metre long and 30 kilograms in weight when it came out of its egg!

The end for the dinosaurs

173 **All dinosaurs on Earth died out by 65 million years ago.** There are dinosaur fossils in the rocks up to this time, but there are none after. However, there are fossils of other creatures like fish, insects, birds and mammals. What happened to wipe out some of the biggest, most numerous and most successful animals the world has ever seen? There are many ideas. It could have been one disaster, or a combination of several.

174 **The dinosaurs may have been killed by a giant lump of rock, a meteorite.** This would have come from outer space and smashed into the Earth. A meteorite would have thrown up vast clouds of water, rocks, ash and dust that blotted out the Sun for many years. Lack of sunlight would mean that plants could not grow so plant-eating dinosaurs died out. Meat-eating dinosaurs had no food so they died as well.

177 It might be that dinosaur eggs were eaten by a plague of animals. Small, shrew-like mammals were around at the time. They may have eaten the eggs at night as the dinosaurs slept.

175 Many volcanoes around the Earth could have erupted all at the same time. This would have thrown out red-hot rocks, ash, dust and clouds of poison gas. Dinosaurs would have choked and died in the gloom.

176 Dinosaurs might have been killed by a disease. This could have gradually spread among all the dinosaurs and killed them off.

METEORITE SMASH!

You will need:
plastic bowl
cooking flour
large pebble
desk light

a place where a mess does not matter!

Ask an adult for help. Put the flour in the bowl. This is Earth's surface. Place the desk light so it shines over the top of the bowl. This is the Sun. The pebble is the meteorite from space. WHAM! Drop the pebble into the bowl. See how the tiny bits of flour float in the air like a mist, making the 'Sun' dimmer. A real meteorite smash may have been the beginning of the end for the dinosaurs.

After the dinosaurs

178 From 65 million years ago there were no dinosaurs left.
Dinosaurs were not the only group of animals to perish at that time. The flying reptiles called pterosaurs, the swimming reptiles, ichthyosaurs and plesiosaurs, also died. When a group of living things dies out completely, this is known as extinction. When many groups of living things all disappear at about the same time, this is a mass extinction.

Diatryma, a giant flightless bird

179 Even though many kinds of animals and plants died out 65 million years ago, many other groups lived on. Insects, worms, fish, birds and mammals all survived the mass extinction – and these groups are still alive today.

180 Even though the dinosaurs and many other reptiles died out in the mass extinction, several groups of reptiles did not. Crocodiles, turtles and tortoises, lizards and snakes all survived. Why some kinds of reptiles like dinosaurs died out in the mass extinction, yet other types did not still puzzles dinosaur experts today.

▼ The mass extinction of 65 million years ago killed the dinosaurs and many other kinds of animals and plants. But plenty of living things survived, as shown here.

Hesperocyon　　　　*Hyracotherium*

181 After the mass extinction, two main groups of animals began to take the place of the dinosaurs and spread over the land. These were birds and mammals. No longer were mammals small and skulking, coming out only after dark when the dinosaurs were asleep. The mammals changed or evolved to become bigger, with many kinds from peaceful plant eaters to huge, fierce predators.

I DON'T BELIEVE IT!

The earliest birds had wings and flapped through the skies. But many of the birds that appeared after the dinosaurs could not fly!

Myths and mistakes

182 As far as we can tell from the clues we have, some of the ideas which have grown up about dinosaurs are **not true.** For example, dinosaurs are shown in different colours such as brown or green. Some have patches or stripes. But no one knows the true colours of dinosaurs. There are a few fossils of dinosaur skin. But being fossils, these have turned to stone and so they are the colour of stone. They are no longer the colour of the original dinosaur skin.

◄ We really have no idea what colour the dinosaurs were. We can guess by looking at reptiles today, but they could have been any colour!

◄ This is a fossil of the skin of *Edmontosaurus*. You can see the texture of the skin, but the only colour is of the rock.

183 Similarly, for many years people thought that all dinosaurs were slow and stupid animals. But they were not. Some dinosaurs were quick and agile. Also some, like *Troodon*, had big brains for their body size. They may have been quite 'clever'.

▲ *Troodon* had a large brain for its body size, almost the same as a monkey of today.

184

Scientists began to study fossils of dinosaurs about 160 years ago, in the 19th century. The first dinosaurs to be studied were very big, such as *Megalosaurus*, *Iguanodon* and *Plateosaurus*. So the idea grew up that all dinosaurs were huge. But they were not. *Compsognathus*, one of the smallest dinosaurs, was only 75 centimetres long – about as big as a pet cat of today.

◀ *Compsognathus* weighed only 3 kilograms and lived 155 million years ago in Europe.

◀ Its name means 'elegant jaw'. Its teeth were small and spaced apart from each other. This makes it likely that *Compsognathus* ate small reptiles and insects, rather than attacking large prey.

▲ These *Wannanosaurus* are using their bony skull caps to fight over territory, food or a mate. The battle is fierce, but *Wannanosaurus* was only about 60 centimetres long! It lived in Asia about 85 million years ago.

I DON'T BELIEVE IT!

One dinosaur's thumb was put on its nose! When scientists first dug up fossils of *Iguanodon*, they found a bone shaped like a horn, as if for *Iguanodon's* nose. Most scientists now believe that the spike was a thumb-claw.

185

Another idea grew up that early cave people had to fight against dinosaurs and kill them – or the other way around. But they did not. There was a very long gap, more than 60 million years, between the very last of the dinosaurs and the earliest people.

186

Some people believe that dinosaurs may survive today in remote, faraway places on Earth, such as thick jungle or ocean islands. But most of the Earth has now been visited and explored, and no living dinosaurs have been seen.

How do we know?

187 We know about dinosaurs mainly from their fossils. Fossils took thousands or millions of years to form. Most fossils form on the bottoms of lakes, rivers or seas, where sand and mud can quickly cover them over and begin to preserve them. If the animal is on dry land, they are more likely to be eaten, or simply to rot away to nothing.

▲ Fossils take millions of years to form. Firstly, an animal, like this trilobite dies. Trilobites lived in the sea about 600 million years ago, long before the first dinosaurs.

▼ Stegoceras was a pachycephalosaur or 'bone-head' dinosaur. It had a very thick layer of bone on top of its head, like an armoured helmet. Its name means 'horny roof'!

Stegoceras was 2 metres long. We can tell from its teeth that it was a herbivore, or plant eater. We can tell roughly the date of the rocks in which the fossil was preserved, so can tell that it lived 70 million years ago on the west coast of what is now North America. Like many plant eaters, it probably lived in a large herd.

188 The body parts most likely to fossilize were the hardest ones, which rot away most slowly after death. These included animal parts such as bones, teeth, horns, claws and shells, and plant parts such as bark, seeds and cones.

Stegoceras had long hind legs, with four toes on each foot. Its front legs were much shorter, and had five toes.

189 Very rarely, a dinosaur or other living thing was buried soon after it died. Then a few of the softer body parts also became fossils, such as bits of skin or the remains of the last meal in the stomach.

1. The soft parts rot away.

2. The remaining shell is buried in mud.

3. The mud turns to rock, which turns the shell to rock, and makes a fossil.

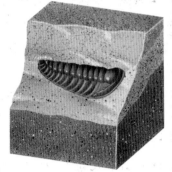

The skull of *Stegoceras* was dome-shaped. The thickest part of the bony plate was 6 centimetres thick, and it protected the brain.

▼ *Stegoceras* may have had head-butting contests with rivals at breeding time, like male sheep and goats do today.

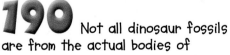

191 **Dinosaur droppings also formed fossils!** They have broken bits of food inside, showing what the dinosaur ate. Some dinosaur droppings are as big as a TV set!

190 **Not all dinosaur fossils are from the actual bodies of dinosaurs.** Some are the signs, traces or remains that they left while alive. These include eggshells, nests, tunnels, footprints, and claw and teeth marks on food.

QUIZ

What formed fossils?

Which body parts of a dinosaur were most likely to become fossils? Remember, fossils form from the hardest, toughest bits that last long enough to become buried in the rocks and turned to stone.

Skull bone   Blood
Muscle   Claws
Leg bone   Eye
Scaly skin   Teeth

Answers:
Skull bone, leg bone, teeth, claws are most likely to form fossils

Digging up dinosaurs

192 Every year, thousands of dinosaur fossils are discovered. Most of them are from dinosaurs already known to scientists. But five or ten might be from new kinds of dinosaurs. From the fossils, scientists try to work out what the dinosaur looked like and how it lived, all those millions of years ago.

▼ These are paleontologists, scientists that look for and study dinosaur bones, uncovering a new skeleton.

193 Most dinosaur fossils are found by hard work. Fossil experts called paleontologists study the rocks in a region and decide where fossils are most likely to occur. They spend weeks chipping and digging the rock. They look closely at every tiny piece to see if it is part of a fossil. However some dinosaur fossils are found by luck. People out walking in the countryside come across a fossil tooth or bone by chance. What a discovery!

194 Finding all the fossils of a single dinosaur, neatly in position as in life, is very rare indeed. Usually only a few fossil parts are found from each dinosaur. These are nearly always jumbled up and broken.

People dig carefully into the rock with hammers, picks and brushes.

Scientists make notes, sketches and photographs, to record every stage of the fossil 'dig'.

195

The fossils are taken back to the paleontology laboratory. They are cleaned and laid out to see which parts are which. It is like trying to put together a jigsaw, with most of the pieces missing. Even those which remain are bent and torn. The fossils are put back together, then soft body parts that did not form fossils, such as skin, are added. Scientists use clues from similar animals alive today, such as crocodiles, to help 'rebuild' the dinosaur.

▲ Cleaning fossils

▲ Laying out fossils

▲ A rebuilt skeleton is displayed in a museum.

Fossils are solid rock and very heavy, but also brittle and easy to crack. So they may need to be wrapped in a strong casing such as plaster-of-paris or glass-fibre.

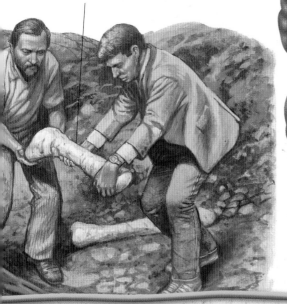

QUIZ

1. What do we call a scientist that studies fossils?

2. How is a fossil 'dig' recorded?

3. How are fossils packed to protect them?

4. What animals can scientists compare dinosaurs fossils with?

Answers:
1. A Paleontologist 2. Notes, sketches and photographs 3. They are put in plaster-of-paris or glass-fibre 4. Crocodiles

Finding new dinosaurs

196 The first fossils of dinosaurs to be studied by scientists came from Europe and North America. However, since those early discoveries in the 1830s and 1840s, dinosaur fossils have been found all over the world.

NORTH AMERICA
EUROPE
CHINA
AFRICA
SOUTH AMERICA
AUSTRALIA

Caudipteryx

Protoarchaeopteryx

197 Some of the most exciting fossils from recent years are being found in China. They include *Caudipteryx*, *Protoarchaeopteryx* and *Sinosauropteryx*. Tiny details of the fossils show that these strange creatures may have had feathers. Today, any creature with feathers is a bird. So were they birds? Or were they dinosaurs with feathers? Nobody knows yet!

Sinosauropteryx

198 Many more exciting finds are being made in Australia, Africa and South America. The small plant eater *Leaellynasaura*, about 2 metres long and one metre tall, lived in Australia 110 million years ago. It may have slept through a cold, snowy winter. Fossils of giant sauropod dinosaurs such as *Jobaria* and *Janenschia* have been uncovered in Africa. In South America there are fossil finds of the biggest plant eaters and meat eaters, such as *Argentinosaurus* and *Giganotosaurus*.

▶ *Jobaria* and *Janenschia* are two giant sauropod dinosaurs from Africa.

199
Some people believe that one day, dinosaurs may be brought back to life. This has already happened – but only in stories, such as the Jurassic Park films. However scientists are trying to obtain genetic material, the chemical called DNA, from fossils. The genetic material may contain the 'instructions' for how a dinosaur grew and lived.

200
Dinosaurs lived and died long, long ago. Their world has been and gone, and cannot alter. But what is changing is our knowledge of the dinosaurs. Every year we know more about them. One sure thing about dinosaurs is that what we know now, will change in the future.

▲ *Leaellynasaura* was discovered in 1989, in a place called 'Dinosaur Cove' near Melbourne, Australia. The scientists who found its fossils were Pat and Thomas Rich .

I DON'T BELIEVE IT!

One dinosaur is named after a young girl! *Leaellynasaura* was named after the daughter of the scientists who found its fossils!

Long, long ago

201 **The Earth was once covered by huge sheets of ice.** This happened several times during Earth's history and we call these frozen times ice ages. However, the ice ages are a tiny part of prehistory. Before then, the world was warm and lakes and seas covered the land. Even earlier than this, there was little rain for thousands of years, and the land was covered in deserts. Over millions of years weather and conditions changed. Living things changed too, in order to survive. This change is called 'evolution'.

Woolly rhinoceros

Cave lion

▼ A scene from the last ice age, about 10,000 years ago. Animals grew thick fur coats to protect themselves from the cold. Many animals, such as woolly mammoths, survived on plants such as mosses. Others, such as cave lions, were fierce hunters, needing meat to survive.

Aurochs

Woolly mammoth

Megaloceros

Life begins

202 **Life began a very, very long time ago.** We know this from the remains of prehistoric life forms that died and were buried. Over millions of years, their remains turned into shapes in rocks, called fossils. The first fossils are over 3000 million years old. They are tiny 'blobs' called bacteria – living things that still survive today.

▼ Fossils of *Anomalocaris* have been found in Canada. It had a circular mouth and finlike body parts. Its body was covered by a shell.

203 **The first plants were seaweeds, which appeared about 1000 million years ago.** Unlike bacteria and blue-green algae, which each had just one living cell, these plants had thousands of cells. Some seaweeds were many metres long. They were called algae – the same name that scientists use today.

204 **By about 800 million years ago, some plants were starting to grow on land.** They were mixed with other living things called moulds, or fungi. Together, the algae (plants) and fungi formed flat green-and-yellow crusts that crept over rocks and soaked up rain. They were called lichens. These still grow on rocks and trees today.

Jellyfish

205 The first animals lived in the
sea – and they were as soft as jelly!
Over 600 million years ago, some of the first
animals were jellyfish, floating in the
water. On the seabed lived groups of soft,
feathery-looking creatures called *Charnia*.
This animal was an early type of coral.
Animals need to take in food by eating
other living things. *Charnia* caught tiny
plants in its 'feathers'.

◀ *Charnia* looked like a prehistoric
plant, but it was actually an animal!

Charnia

206 One of the first hunting
animals was *Anomalocaris*. It lived
520 million years ago, swimming
through the sea in search of prey.
It caught smaller creatures in its
pincers, then pushed them into
its mouth. *Anomalocaris* was a
cousin of crabs and insects.
It was one of the biggest
hunting animals of its
time, even though it was
only 60 centimetres long.

▲ The *Cooksonia* plant had forked stems
that carried water. The earliest
examples have been found in Ireland.

207 By 400 million years ago, plants on
land were growing taller. They had stiff stems that
held them upright and carried water to their
topmost parts. An early upright plant was *Cooksonia*.
It was the tallest living thing on land, yet it was only
5 centimetres high – hardly the size of your thumb!

Animals swarm the seas

208
Some of the first common animals were worms. However, they were not earthworms in soil. At the time there was no soil and the land was bare. These worms lived in the sea. They burrowed in mud for plants and animals to eat.

◄ *Ottoia* was a sea worm that fed by filtering tiny food particles from the sea.

▼ Trilobites moved quickly across the seabed. Some could roll up into a ball like woodlice do today. This was a means of protection.

209
The next animals to become common were trilobites. They first lived about 550 million years ago in the sea. Trilobites crawled along the seabed eating tiny bits of food they found. Their name means 'three lobes' (parts). A trilobite had two grooves along its back, from head to tail, so its body had three main parts – left, middle and centre.

▼ *Pterygotus* was a fierce hunter, with large eyes and long claws.

210
Trilobites were some of the first animals with legs that bent at the joints. Animals with jointed legs are called arthropods. They have been the most common creatures for millions of years, including trilobites long ago, and later on, crabs, spiders and insects. Like other arthropods, trilobites had a tough, outer shell for protection.

211
Some of the first hunters were sea scorpions – some were as big as lions! *Pterygotus* was 2 metres long. It swished its tail to chase prey through water, which it tore apart with its huge claws. Sea scorpions lived 500 to 250 million years ago. Unlike modern scorpions, they had no sting in their tails.

212 For millions of years the seabed was covered with the curly shells of ammonites. Some of these shells were as small as your fingernail, others were bigger than dinner plates. Ammonites were successful creatures and thousands of kinds survived for millions of years. Each ammonite had big eyes to see prey and long tentacles (arms) to catch it with. Ammonites died out at the same time as the dinosaurs, around 65 million years ago.

▲ This rock contains an ammonite fossil. The shell would have protected the soft-bodied creature inside.

◄ *Pikaia* looked a little bit like an eel with fins.

213 Among the worms, trilobites and ammonites was a small creature that had a very special body part – the beginnings of a backbone. It was called *Pikaia* and lived about 530 million years ago. Gradually, more animals with backbones, called vertebrates, evolved from it. Today, vertebrates rule much of the world – they are fish, reptiles, birds and mammals.

QUIZ
1. Did sea scorpions have stings in their tails?
2. What does the name 'trilobite' mean?
3. What kind of animal was *Ottoia*?
4. When did ammonites die out?
5. What was special about *Pikaia*?

Answers:
1. No 2. Three lobes, or parts
3. A worm 4. 65 million years ago
5. It had an early type of backbone

Very fishy

214 **The first fish could not bite — they were suckers!** About 500 million years ago, new animals appeared in the sea — the first fish. They had no jaws or teeth and probably sucked in worms and small pieces of food from the mud.

▲ *Hemicyclaspis* was an early jawless fish. It had eyes on top of its head and probably lived on the seabed. This way it could keep a look out for predators above.

215 **Some early fish wore suits of armour!** They had hard, curved plates of bone all over their bodies for protection. These fish were called placoderms and most were fierce hunters. Some had huge jaws with sharp sheets of bone for slicing up prey.

216 **Spiny sharks had spines, but they were not really sharks.** These fish were similar in shape to today's sharks, but they lived in rivers and lakes, not the sea, about 430 million years ago. *Climatius* was a spiny shark that looked fierce, but it was only as big as your finger!

◀ The fins on the back of *Climatius* were supported by needle-sharp spines. These helped to protect it from attacks by squid or other fish.

217
The first really big hunting fish was bigger than today's great white shark! *Dunkleosteus* grew to almost 10 metres long and swam in the oceans 360 million years ago. It sliced up prey, such as other fish, using its massive teeth made of narrow blades of bone, each one as big as this book.

218
Some early fish started to 'walk' out of water. Types of fish called lobefins appeared 390 million years ago. Their side fins each had a 'stump' at the base made of muscle. If the water in their pool dried up, lobefins could use their fins like stubby legs to waddle over land to another pool. *Eusthenopteron* was a lobefin fish about 1.2 metres long. Over millions of years, some lobefins evolved into four-legged animals called tetrapods.

VERY FISHY!
You will need:
waxed card (like the kind used to make milk cartons) crayons scissors piece of soap

Place the piece of waxed card face down. Fold the card up at the edges. Draw a fish on the card. Cut a small notch in the rear of the card and wedge the piece of soap in it. Put the 'fish' in a bath of cold water and watch it swim away.

▼ *Eusthenopteron* could clamber about on dry land when moving from one stretch of water to another.

Animals invade the land

219 **The first land animals lived about 450 million years ago.** These early creatures, which came from the sea, were arthropods – creatures with hard outer body casings and jointed legs. They included prehistoric insects, spiders and millipedes. *Arthropleura* was a millipede – it was 2 metres in length!

▶ *Arthropleura* was as long as a human and was the largest-ever land arthropod.

220 **Some amphibians were fierce hunters.** *Gerrothorax* was about one metre long and spent most of its time at the bottom of ponds or streams. Its eyes pointed upward, to see fish swimming past, just above. *Gerrothorax* would then jump up to grab the fish in its wide jaws.

221 **The first four-legged animal had eight toes on each front foot!** *Acanthostega* used its toes to grip water plants as it swam. It lived about 380 million years ago and was one metre long. Creatures like it soon began to walk on land, too. They were called tetrapods, which means 'four legs'. They were a big advance in evolution – the first land animals with backbones.

◀ *Acanthostega* probably spent most of its time in water. It had gills for breathing underwater as well as lungs for breathing air.

223 Soon four-legged animals called amphibians were racing across the land. Amphibians were the first backboned animals to move fast out of the water. *Aphaneramma* had long legs and could run quickly. However, prehistoric amphibians, like those of today such as frogs and newts, had to return to the water to lay their eggs.

222 Fins became legs for walking on land, and tails changed, too. As the fins of lobefin fish evolved into legs, their tails became longer and more muscular. *Ichthyostega* had a long tail with a fin along its upper side. This tail design was good for swimming in water, and also helpful when wriggling across a swamp.

224 Some amphibians grew as big as crocodiles! *Eogyrinus* was almost 5 metres long and had strong jaws and teeth, like a crocodile. However, it lived about 300 million years ago, long before any crocodiles appeared. Although *Eogyrinus* could walk on dry land, it spent most of its time in streams and swamps.

◄ *Ichthyostega* had short legs, so it could probably only move slowly on land.

Life after death

225 **There were times in prehistory when almost everything died out.** These times are called mass extinctions. Just a few types of plants and animals survive, which can then change, or evolve, into new kinds. A mass extinction about 290 million years ago allowed a fairly new group of animals to spread fast – the reptiles.

226 **Reptiles' skin and eggs helped them to survive.** Unlike an amphibian's, a reptile's scaly skin was waterproof. Also, the jelly-like eggs of amphibians had to be laid in water, while a reptile's eggs had tough shells for surviving on land. Around 280 million years ago, reptiles such as 1.5 metre-long *Varanosaurus* were spreading to dry areas where amphibians could not survive.

EDIBLE REPTILES

You will need:
100 grams dried milk
100 grams smooth peanut butter   2 tablespoons honey
currants   food colouring

Mix the dried milk, peanut butter and honey in a bowl. Mould this paste into reptile shapes. Decorate with currants for eyes and add food colouring for bright skin patterns. Then cause a mass extinction – eat them!

▲ *Varanosaurus* lived in what is now Texas, USA, and may have hunted fish in swamps.

▶ *Hylonomus* lived in forests in what is now Canada. It hunted insects, spiders and millipedes.

227 The first reptile looked like a lizard.

However *Hylonomus* belonged to a different reptile group to lizards. It lived like a lizard, chasing prey on the ground and in trees. It lived 345 million years ago.

228 Some reptiles started to avoid bad weather by sleeping underground. *Diictodon* lived

about 260 million years ago and used its large teeth to chop up tough plant food. It may have dug holes to shelter from the heat, cold and rain.

▼ *Diictodon* had strong legs and sharp claws for burrowing.

Wars around the world

▼ The nostrils and eyes of *Mastodonsaurus* were on top of its head so that it could breathe and look around whilst hiding underwater.

229 **Some amphibians fought back against the reptiles.** *Mastodonsaurus* was a big, strong amphibian, 2 metres long, with sharp teeth. It hunted fish, other amphibians, and small reptiles. It lived at a time when reptiles were spreading even faster, about 250 to 203 million years ago. But most other big amphibians did not survive the reptiles.

230 **Other amphibians managed to survive the reptile takeover, too.** They were mainly small and hid in water or swamps. One was *Branchiosaurus*, which was about 12 centimetres long and hunted small fish in ponds.

▲ *Lystrosaurus* lived in Antarctica when it was a land of lush, tropical plant life. Today it is a frozen continent, covered by thick ice.

231 **Reptiles showed how the world's lands moved about.** *Lystrosaurus* lived about 200 million years ago and its fossils come from Europe, Asia, Africa and Antarctica. This reptile could not swim, so all of these landmasses, or continents, must have been joined together at one time. Over millions of years, they drifted apart to form today's positions.

232 **Some plant-eating reptiles had very sharp teeth.** *Moschops* was as big as a rhino and lived in southern Africa about 270 million years ago. Its teeth were long and straight, and ended with a sharp edge like a chisel. *Moschops* could easily bite tough leaves and twigs off bushes.

▼ As well as sharp teeth, *Moschops* had very strong skull bones, so it may have head-butted rivals in fights.

Reptiles take over

233 Reptiles don't like to be too hot, or too cold. Otherwise they may overheat, or be too cold to move. Most reptiles bask in sunshine to get warm, then stay in the shade. *Dimetrodon* was a fierce reptile. It had a large 'sail' of skin on its back to soak up heat from the sun.

▲ The name *Dimetrodon* means 'two-types-of-teeth'. It was given this name as it had stabbing teeth and slicing teeth. It measured 3 metres in length.

QUIZ
1. How did *Dimetrodon* get warm?
2. Which types of reptile evolved into mammals?
3. How did some early reptiles swim?
4. Did the first crocodiles like water?

Answers:
1. By basking in the sun
2. Therapsids 3. By swishing their tails from side to side 4. No, they hated it!

234 The first crocodiles hated water! An early type of crocodile, *Protosuchus*, stayed on land. It lived in North America about 190 million years ago. It was one metre long and could run across dry land when hunting, using its long legs.

▶ *Protosuchus* had very powerful jaw muscles to snap its teeth shut on prey.

▶ *Chasmatosaurus* had teeth on the roof of its mouth as well as in its jaws.

235 Some reptiles moved by using their tails.

Many types of early reptiles had long, strong tails. They probably lived in water and swished their tails to push themselves along. *Chasmatosaurus* was 2 metres long and probably hunted for fish. It looked like a crocodile but was more closely related to the dinosaurs.

236 Some reptiles began to look very much like mammals.

Cynognathus was as big as a large dog, and instead of scaly skin it had fur. It belonged to a group of reptiles called therapsids. Around 220 million years ago, some types of small therapsids were evolving into the first mammals.

◀ The jaws of *Cynognathus* were so powerful they could bite through bone. Its name means 'dog jaw'.

Living with the dinosaurs

237 Some reptiles were as big and fierce as dinosaurs – but they lived in the sea. One of these was *Mosasaurus*. It grew up to 10 metres in length and may have weighed 10 tonnes, far bigger than today's great white shark.

238 One sea reptile had teeth the size of saucers! The huge, round, flat teeth of *Placodus* were more than 10 centimetres across. It used them to crush shellfish and sea urchins. *Placodus* was 2 metres long and lived at the same time as the first dinosaurs, about 230 million years ago.

I DON'T BELIEVE IT!
Fossils of Mosasaurus were found in the same place over 200 years apart! The first was found in a quarry in the Netherlands in 1780. The second was found in the same place in 1998.

▼ *Mosasaurus* was a huge sea reptile. It had razor-sharp teeth and could swim with speed to catch its prey.

▼ *Archaeopteryx* had a long bony tail, unlike modern birds, which have no bones in their tails.

239 Fossils of the first bird were mistaken for a dinosaur. *Archaeopteryx* lived in Europe about 155 million years ago. Some of its fossils look very similar to the fossils of small dinosaurs. So *Archaeopteryx* was thought to be a dinosaur, until scientists saw the faint shape of its feathers and realized it was a bird.

240 Soon there were many kinds of birds flying above the dinosaurs. *Confuciusornis* was about 60 centimetres long and lived in what is now China, 120 million years ago. It had a backwards-pointing big toe on each foot, which suggests it climbed through the trees. It is also the earliest-known bird to have a true beak.

▲ Fossils of *Confuciusornis* have been found in China. It is named after the famous Chinese wise man, Confucius.

241 Mammals lived at the same time as dinosaurs. These animals have warm blood, and fur or hair, unlike a reptile's scaly skin. *Megazostrodon* was the earliest mammal known to scientists. It lived in southern Africa about 215 million years ago – only 15 million years or so after the dinosaurs began life on Earth. It was just 12 centimetres long, and probably hunted insects.

▼ *Megazostrodon* probably came out at night to hunt for its insect prey. It looked a little like a modern-day shrew.

In and over the sea

242 One prehistoric reptile had the bendiest neck ever!
The sea reptile *Elasmosaurus* had a neck over 5 metres long – the same as three people lying head-to-toe. Its neck was so bendy that *Elasmosaurus* could twist it around in a circle as it looked for fish and other creatures to eat.

243 The first big flying animals were not birds, but pterosaurs.
They lived at the same time as the dinosaurs, and died out at the same time too, about 65 million years ago. *Pteranodon* was one of the later pterosaurs and lived about 70 million years ago. It swooped over the sea to scoop up fish.

▼ *Pteranodon* scoops up prey while long-necked *Elasmosaurus* snaps its jaws in search of food.

Pteranodon

244 The largest flying animal of all time was as big as a plane! With wings measuring up to 14 metres from tip to tip, the pterosaur *Quetzalcoatlus* was twice as big as any flying bird. It may have lived like a vulture, soaring high in the sky, and then landing to peck at a dead body of a dinosaur.

245 Some fossils of sea creatures are found thousands of kilometres from the sea. Around 100 to 70 million years ago, much of what is now North America was flooded. The shallow waters teemed with all kinds of fish, reptiles and other creatures. Today their fossils are found on dry land.

Elasmosaurus

After the dinosaurs

246 A disaster about 65 million years ago killed off the dinosaurs and many other creatures. The main new group of animals was the mammals. Most were small, like rats and mice. *Leptictidium* lived 50 to 40 million years ago. It may be related to moles and shrews.

▲ *Leptictidium* probably hopped like a kangaroo!

248 Often the name of a prehistoric animal can be misleading, like *Palaeotherium*, which simply means 'ancient animal'. However this name was given over 200 years ago, in 1804, because scientists of the time did not know as much as modern scientists. Later studies show that *Palaeotherium* was one of the first animals in the group of hoofed mammals that includes horses.

◀ *Pakicetus* is the earliest-known whale.

247 Whales began life on dry land and gradually returned to the sea. *Pakicetus* lived about 50 million years ago and was nearly 2 metres long. It probably spent alot of time on land as well as in water.

▼ A mother *Uintatherium* and her baby. This strange-looking creature was the largest land animal of its time. Its head was covered in horns and it had small tusks.

249
Around 40 million years ago, the largest animal walking the Earth was *Uintatherium*. This plant eater was over 3 metres long and nearly 2 metres tall at the shoulder – about the same size as a cow. Its fossils were found near the Uinta River in Colorado, USA. *Uintatherium* is thought to be a cousin of horses and elephants.

250
An animal's looks can be misleading. *Patriofelis* means 'father of the cats'. It lived 45 million years ago and was named because scientists thought it looked like an early cat. Later they realized that it merely looked like a cat. It was really a member of an extinct group of hunting animals called creodonts.

QUIZ
1. What does the name *Patriofelis* mean?
2. How long was *Pakicetus*?
3. In what year were *Palaeotherium* fossils found?
4. How tall was *Uintatherium*?
5. When did dinosaurs die out and mammals start to take over?

Answers:
1. 'Father of the cats'
2. About 2 metres 3. 1804
4. Almost 2 metres tall at the shoulder
5. 65 million years ago

As the world cooled down

251 Before the world started to cool 30 million years ago, palm trees grew almost everywhere — but they became rare. These trees had thrived in warm, wet conditions. But as Earth cooled, other plants took over, such as magnolias, pines, oaks and birch. These changes meant that animals changed too.

▼ *Brontotherium* was somewhere in size between a rhino and an elephant. Males used the Y-shaped horn on their snouts in fighting competitions.

252 *Pyrotherium* means 'fire beast', but not because this plant eater could walk through fire. Its fossils were found in layers of ash from an ancient volcano in Argentina, South America. The volcano probably erupted, and its fumes and ash suffocated and burned all the animals nearby. *Pyrotherium* was about as big as a cow and looked like a combination of a pig and a short-tusked elephant.

253 Many prehistoric animals have exciting names — *Brontotherium* means 'thunder beast'. Where the fossils of *Brontotherium* were found in North America, local people thought they were bones of the gods. They thought that these gods rode chariots across the sky and started thunderstorms, which led to the animal's name.

254 **Andrewsarchus was a real big-head!** At one metre long, it had the biggest head of any hunting mammal on land, and its strong jaws were filled with sharp, pointed teeth. Its whole body was bigger than a tiger of today. *Andrewsarchus* probably lived like a hyena, crunching up bones and gristle from dead animals. Yet it belonged to a mammal group that was mostly plant eaters. It lived 30 million years ago in what is now the deserts of Mongolia, Asia.

▲ *Andrewsarchus* was the biggest meat-eating land animal ever to have lived.

QUIZ
1. What does *Brontotherium* mean?
2. What does *Pyrotherium* mean?
3. How long was the head of *Andrewsarchus*?
4. Where did *Arsinoitherium* live?

Answers:
1. 'Thunder beast' 2. 'Fire beast' 3. One metre 4. Northern Africa

255 **Some animals had horns as tall as people!** *Arsinoitherium's* two massive horns looked like powerful weapons – but they were light, fragile and made of very thin bone. This plant eater lived in northern Africa about 35 million years ago. It was almost as big as an elephant and may have been an ancient cousin of the elephant group.

▲ The horns on *Arsinoitherium's* head were hollow and may have been used to make mating calls.

What fossils tell us

256 Fossils are the remains of animals or plants that have been preserved in rock. Usually only the hard parts of an animal, such as teeth or bones, are preserved in this way. Trilobites had a tough, outer skeleton so usually only this part of their body is found as a fossil. Scientists use the fossil to try to create a picture of how the soft parts, such as muscles and organs, may have looked.

▼ Some early humans are known only from their fossil footprints, not from fossils of their bones. These footprints were discovered in 1978 in Tanzania, Africa.

▲ By examining trilobite fossils, scientists were able to tell that this animal could see in all directions.

257 Some fossils are known as trace fossils. These are not fossilized parts of an animal's body, such as bones, but preserved marks left behind by the animal, such as footprints or droppings. By studying the fossilized footprints of an extinct animal, scientists can discover how it walked, how fast it could move and whether it lived alone or in groups.

258

On rare occasions the softer parts of an animal may be preserved as well as the hard parts. Insects may become trapped in sticky sap oozing from pine trees. This sap may then become fossilized as amber, with the insect caught inside. Scientists have found hundreds of insects, spiders and other small creatures perfectly preserved in this way.

▲ Amber spider fossils show that spiders have changed little over the last 30 million years.

◄ Some fossils of *Archaeopteryx* are so well preserved that even the feathers can be seen.

259

One of the most important and valuable fossils ever found was of *Archaeopteryx*, in Germany in 1860. The fossil is about 150 million years old and shows a creature that looked part dinosaur and part bird. It had the feathers and wings of a bird, but the teeth and bony tail of a dinosaur. This shows that birds probably evolved from a type of dinosaur.

260

The importance of some fossils can be misunderstood. *Acanthostega* was one of the very earliest amphibian fossils ever found. However, the man who found the fossil was not an expert on amphibians. When his expedition returned from Greenland, the fossil was put in a drawer at a museum. It was not until over 30 years later that an expert on amphibians happened to see the fossil and realized how important it was.

Prehistoric prowlers

261 Some animals probably ate just about anything. Entelodonts were piglike animals that lived about 25 million years ago. *Dinohyus* was one of the largest entelodonts. Its teeth were sharp and strong, and it had powerful jaw muscles. It ate almost anything from leaves, roots and seeds, to small animals.

262 Some predators (hunting animals) walked on tiptoe but others were flat-footed. Most mammal predators, such as cats and dogs, walk on the ends of their toes. This helps them to run faster. *Daphoenodon* walked on flat feet, like a bear. It is often called a 'bear-dog' as it looked like a dog but walked like a bear.

▼ *Dinohyus* lived in North America and grew to be about 3 metres long. Its powerful neck muscles and large canine teeth suggest it could have broken bones and eaten flesh.

263 Fossils can show if predators hunted by day or at night. *Plesictis* was 75 centimetres long and its fossils show it had large sockets (spaces) for its eyes. This means that it probably hunted at night. It also had sharp claws and a long tail, so it probably scampered through trees hunting birds and insects, gripping with its claws and balancing with its tail.

264 Some predators have changed little over millions of years. *Potamotherium* was an early otter and lived in Europe, 23 million years ago. It looked almost like the otters of today. Its shape was so well-suited to hunting fish in streams that it has hardly changed.

QUIZ
1. Why is *Daphoenodon* sometimes called a 'bear-dog'?
2. Which hunter was active at night?
3. What prey did *Potamotherium* eat?
4. What do scientists think *Entelodon* ate?

Answers:
1. Because it looked like a dog, but walked like a bear 2. *Plesictis* 3. Fish 4. Almost anything

▲ *Potamotherium* had a bendy backbone to allow it to twist about in the water.

119

Amazing ancient elephants

265 **The first elephant had tiny tusks and almost no trunk.** *Moeritherium* lived in northern Africa about 36 million years ago. It stood just 60 centimetres tall and may have weighed around 20 kilograms – about the size of a large pet dog.

I DON'T BELIEVE IT!

The tusks of *Anancus* were over 4 metres long – almost as long as the animal itself.

▶ Woolly mammoths had coats of shaggy hair. This hair kept their warm inner fur dry and waterproof in the freezing conditions of the ice age.

266 **Some elephants were very hairy.** The woolly mammoth was covered in thick, long dense hair to keep out the cold of the ice age. It was larger than a modern elephant and was probably hunted by early people. The last woolly mammoths may have died out less than 10,000 years ago.

267 **One elephant had tusks like shovels.** *Platybelodon* lived about nine million years ago in Europe, Asia and Africa. Its lower tusks were shaped like broad, flat shovels. Perhaps it used them to scoop up water plants to eat.

268 **Some elephants had four tusks.** *Tetralophodon* lived about eight million years ago and stood 3 metres tall. Its fossils have been found in Europe, Asia, Africa and America, so it was a very widespread and successful animal.

269 **The biggest elephant was the Columbian mammoth.** It stood 4 metres tall and may have weighed over 10 tonnes – twice as much as most elephants today. It lived on the grasslands of southern North America.

▼ The Columbian mammoth had tusks that twisted into curved, spiral shapes.

270 **Elephants were more varied and common long ago, than they are today.** *Anancus* roamed Europe and Asia two million years ago. Like modern elephants, it used its trunk to pull leaves from branches and its tusks to dig up roots. However most kinds of prehistoric elephants died out. Only two kinds survive today, in Africa and Asia.

Animals with hooves

271 **The first horse was hardly larger than a pet cat.** *Hyracotherium* lived in Europe, Asia and North America about 50 million years ago. It was only 20 centimetres tall and lived in woods and forests.

▼ *Hyracotherium* is sometimes called *Eohippus*, which means 'dawn horse'. It had a short neck, slender legs and a long tail.

272 **Early horses did not eat grass — because there wasn't any.** Grasses and open plains did not appear on Earth until 25 million years ago. Then early horses moved onto them, started to eat grass, and gradually became bigger.

273 **Over millions of years, horses gradually lost their toes!** The very first horses had five toes per foot, each ending in a small nail-like hoof. *Hyracotherium* had four toes on each front foot and three on each back foot. Later, *Mesohippus*, which was as big as a labrador dog, had three toes on each foot. Today's horses have just one toe on each foot, which ends in a large hoof.

274

Some prehistoric camels had horns. *Synthetoceras* had a pair of horns at the top of its head, and also an extraordinary Y-shaped horn growing from its nose. It probably used these horns to fight enemies and also to show off to others of its kind at breeding time.

▶ The amazing nose horn of *Synthetoceras* was present only on male animals.

HORSE RACE

You will need:
stiff card crayons scissors string
about 4 metres long

On the card, draw a picture of *Hyracotherium*. Colour it in and cut it out. Make a hole in the middle, about 2 centimetres from the top. Thread the string through the hole and tie one end to a piece of furniture. Pull the string tight, then flick it with a finger to make *Hyracotherium* move along!

◀ *Megaloceros* may have stored food for the winter in the form of fat in a hump on its shoulder.

275

Some prehistoric deer had antlers as big as a person! *Megaloceros* means 'big deer' and it was as big as today's biggest deer, the moose. But its antlers were even bigger, measuring almost 4 metres from tip to tip. *Megaloceros* may have survived in some parts of Europe until as little as 3000 years ago.

Cats, dogs and bears

276 **The sabre-tooth 'tiger' *Smilodon* had two huge sharp teeth like sabres (swords) — but it was not really a tiger.** It belonged to a different group of cats to real tigers. *Smilodon*'s teeth were long and sharp but not very strong. It probably used them like knives to stab and slash at its prey, which then bled to death. *Smilodon* then ate it without a struggle.

▶ *Smilodon* had enormously powerful shoulders, so it may have sprung on its prey and held it down.

277 **The earliest cats were similar to those of today.** *Dinictis* lived about 30 million years ago and was strong and stealthy, like the modern-day cougar (mountain lion). It probably hunted like modern cats too, by creeping up close to a victim, then leaping on it to bite its throat or neck.

278 **The first dog, *Hesperocyon*, had a long body and short legs, more like a stoat or mongoose.** It was about 90 centimetres long and lived about 30 million years ago. Only later dogs had long legs and were able to run fast after their prey.

◀ *Hesperocyon* may have hunted in packs. This would have allowed it to hunt animals much larger than itself.

279

The sabre-tooth 'cat' *Thylacosmilus* was not even a real cat! It had a cat-shaped head, body, legs and tail. Yet it was a marsupial – a cousin of kangaroos and koalas. It lived in South America four million years ago.

280

Sea lions did not develop from lions – but from dogs. *Allodesmus* was an early type of sea lion and lived about 13 million years ago. It had strong flippers for fast swimming. Its fossil bones show that it came originally from the dog group.

I DON'T BELIEVE IT!

Even if global warming continues, the world will not be as hot as it was 35 million years ago.

◄ Early humans had to face many natural dangers, such as cave bears.

281

Early people hunted cave bears, and cave bears hunted early people! The huge cave bear of the Ice Age was as big as today's grizzly bear. Humans called Neanderthals hunted them and used their bones and teeth as ornaments. The bears hunted people too, and left their bones in caves.

Prehistoric giants

282 **The largest flying bird ever was as big as a small plane!** *Argentavis* was twice the size of any flying bird today. Its wings measured 7 metres from tip to tip. It was a huge vulture that fed on the dead bodies of other creatures, tearing off their flesh with its powerful hooked beak.

▼ *Argentavis* lived about seven million years ago in South America.

283 Some birds were even bigger than *Argentavis*, but they could not fly — and they were deadly hunters. In South America about one million years ago, *Titanis* grew to 3 metres tall. It raced after its prey, which it tore apart with its huge, hooked beak.

284 A type of prehistoric kangaroo, *Procoptodon*, was twice as big as those of today. Yet it could bound along as fast as a racehorse. Like kangaroos of today, it was a marsupial, carrying its baby in a pouch. It lived in Australia.

◄ *Titanis* was a monstrous hunting bird that chased after mammals such as this early horse, in South America.

285 The largest land mammal ever to have lived was a type of rhino – without a nose horn.

Paraceratherium was far bigger than an elephant, at 8 metres long and 6 metres tall at the shoulder. It weighed over 15 tonnes – more than three elephants. This giant creature lived in Asia about 30 million years ago and was a peaceful plant eater.

I DON'T BELIEVE IT!

Giant marsupials may have started stories of the 'Bunyip', a mythical Australian animal.

▲ The huge *Paraceratherium* fed by browsing on trees, stripping off the leaves. Even though it was so big and heavy, *Paraceratherium* had long legs, which means it was probably capable of running.

A giant island

286 For almost 50 million years, South America was like a giant island – with many strange animals that were found nowhere else. Until three million years ago, South America was separated from North America by an ocean. On islands, animals can evolve into unusual kinds found nowhere else in the world.

▶ South America was once separated from North America. This meant that certain animals that survived there did not live anywhere else in the world.

287 Elephants were not the only animals with trunks! *Macrauchenia* lived in South America about 100,000 years ago. It was about the size of a camel and probably had a trunk to gather leaves to eat. It was not a type of elephant, but a distant cousin of horses and rhinos.

Macrauchenia

288 When South America joined North America, many kinds of prehistoric animals died out. In particular, animals from North America spread south. They were better at surviving than the South American creatures, and they gradually took over.

289 One South American creature that has died out was the giant sloth, *Megatherium*. It was a cousin of the smaller sloths that live in trees today – but it was far too big to climb trees. At 6 metres long and 3 tonnes in weight, it was the size of an elephant! It may have died out only in the last few thousand years.

290 Armadillos were once nearly as big as tanks! *Glyptodon* was almost 4 metres long and covered in a thick dome of bony armour. It lived in South America until about 10,000 years ago. Today, armadillos are quite small, but they are still covered in bony plates for protection.

Megatherium

Glyptodon

I DON'T BELIEVE IT!
The armadillo is a South American animal that lives in North America, too. Over the past 100 years, it has spread north at a rate of one kilometre every ten years.

Our prehistoric relations

291 Monkeys, apes and humans first appeared over 50 million years ago — the first kinds looked like squirrels. This group is called the primates. *Plesiadapis* was one of the first primates. It lived 55 million years ago in Europe and North America.

◀ *Plesiadapis* had claws on its fingers and toes, unlike monkeys and apes, which had nails.

292 Early apes walked on all fours. About 20 million years ago, *Dryopithecus* lived in Europe and Asia. It used its arms and legs to climb trees. When it came down to the ground, it walked on all fours. It was 60 centimetres long and ate fruit and leaves.

I DON'T BELIEVE IT
The first fossils of the giant ape *Gigantopithecus* to be studied by scientists came from a second-hand shop in Hong Kong, over 70 years ago.

▶ The early ape *Dryopithecus* walked flat on its feet, unlike other apes, which walked on their knuckles.

▼ The need to see longer distances on grasslands may have caused the first apes to walk on two legs.

293 Some kinds of apes may have walked on their two back legs, like us. About 4.5 million years ago *Ardipithecus* lived in Africa. Only a few of its fossils have been found. However, experts think it may have walked upright on its back legs. It could have made the first steps in the change, or evolution, from apes to humans.

294 One prehistoric ape was a real giant — over 3 metres tall! Its name, *Gigantopithecus*, means 'giant ape'. It was much larger than today's biggest ape, the gorilla, which grows to 2 metres tall. *Gigantopithecus* probably ate roots and seeds, and may have hunted small animals such as birds, rats and lizards.

▶ The enormous *Gigantopithecus* could probably stand on its hind legs to reach food.

295 Scientists work out which animals are our closest cousins partly from fossils — and also from chemicals. The chemical called DNA contains genes, which are instructions for how living things grow and work. The living animals with DNA most similar to ours are the great apes, chimpanzees and gorillas, both from Africa. So our ancient cousins were probably apes like them. The orang-utan, from Southeast Asia, is less similar.

The first humans

▼ *Australopithecus* walked upright. It spent most of its days searching for food.

296 Our early prehistoric cousins were much smaller than us. One kind was called *Australopithecus afarensis*, meaning 'southern ape from Afar', because its fossils come from the Afar region of East Africa. It was just over one metre tall, lived over three million years ago, and looked part human and part ape.

297 Very early kinds of humans lived almost two million years ago. They were called *Homo erectus*, which means 'upright human', and they were as tall as us. These first humans spread from Africa, across Asia, and into Europe. However, they all died out about 200,000 years ago.

▶ *Homo erectus* was the first living creature to use fire for cooking and warmth.

298 From one million years ago early people made tools out of stone — they had not invented metal. They chipped rocks like flint to form a sharp, cutting edge, and shaped stones into knives, scrapers, or axes. Stone tools have been found with the bones of animals that were cut up for food, along with the ashes of fires used for cooking — and the bones of the people themselves.

► The Flores humans probably used stone tools to hunt animals such as the pygmy elephant.

299 Some prehistoric animals were domesticated (tamed) to become the first farm animals.

This began around 15,000 years ago. For example, fierce aurochs, a type of wild cow, were gradually bred over time to become quiet, calm animals. They provided people with food and clothing.

300 We are still discovering surprises about prehistoric life.

In 2004, scientists found the bones and tools of tiny humans, less than one metre tall, on the island of Flores in Southeast Asia. Their remains are from over 90,000 to less than 15,000 years old. No one knew they existed. In the future we may discover more amazing finds from the past.

QUIZ

1. Were prehistoric humans big or small?
2. What were the first tools made from?
3. When were animals first domesticated?
4. What was discovered on the island of Flores?

Answers:
1. Small 2. Stone 3. 15,000 years ago 4. Flores man

301 Extinction is when all individuals of one kind of living thing die out forever, so there are no more alive. It usually applies to a whole species (kind) of living thing, not just to one individual. Extinction has happened for billions of years since life on Earth began. Scientists estimate that 999 out of every 1000 kinds of living things that have ever existed have become extinct. Today, the number of extinctions is speeding up because of what people are doing to the natural world.

▼ Giant dragonflies, millipedes as big as dining tables and enormous tree ferns once inhabited forests 300 million years ago. However all of the creatures in this prehistoric swamp have long been extinct.

What is extinction?

302 Extinction is the dying out of a particular kind, or type, of living thing. It is gone forever and can never come back (although this may change in the future). Extinction affects plants such as flowers and trees, as well as fungi such as mushrooms and moulds. It also affects tiny worms and bugs, and big creatures such as dinosaurs and mammoths.

▲ The 'terror bird' *Phorusrhacos* lived ten million years ago. Nothing like it survives today.

303 Extinction is linked to how we classify (group) living things. It usually applies to a species. A species includes all living things that look similar and breed to produce more of their kind. For instance, all lions belong to one species, which scientists call *Panthera leo*.

QUIZ

Which of these could, perhaps, one day become extinct?
1. Great white sharks 2. Robots
3. Daisies 4. Cameras with rolls of film (not digital)
5. Satellites 6. Houseflies

Answers:
Only living things can become extinct, so the answers are 1, 3 and 6

304 One example of an extinct species is the giant elk *Megaloceros giganteus* of the last Ice Age. The last ones died out almost 8000 years ago. But not all elk species became extinct. A similar but separate species, the elk (moose) *Alces alces*, is still alive today.

305

Sometimes extinction affects a subspecies. This is a group of animals within a species that are all very similar, and slightly different from others in the species. All tigers today belong to one species, *Panthera tigris*. There were once eight subspecies of tiger. Two have become extinct in the past 100 years, the Balinese tiger and the Javan tiger.

▶ All six living subspecies of tiger differ slightly – and all are threatened with extinction.

Bengal tiger

South China tiger

▲ The last Balinese tiger, the smallest subspecies, was killed in 1937.

306

Extinction can also affect a group of closely related species, which is called a genus. There have been about ten species of mammoths over the last two million years. They all belonged to the genus *Mammuthus*, including the woolly mammoth and the steppe mammoth. All mammoths have died out, so the genus is extinct.

◀ The Columbian mammoth, one of the biggest in the genus, died out by 12,000 years ago.

Siberian tiger

Sumatran tiger

Malayan tiger

Indochinese tiger

Extinction and evolution

307 Extinctions have happened through billions of years of prehistory as a natural part of evolution. Evolution is the gradual change in living things, resulting in new species appearing. As this happened, other species could not survive and became extinct.

◄ Today's hagfish differ little from their extinct cousins millions of years ago, but they are a separate species.

308 Evolution occurs as the result of changing conditions. Living things adapt to become better suited to conditions as they change, such as the weather and types of habitats (living places).

► Unlike the hagfish, the extinct armoured fish *Hemicyclaspis* from 400 million years ago has no living relatives.

I DON'T BELIEVE IT!

Trilobites were a group of marine creatures that survived for almost 300 million years. Within that time at least 18,000 kinds came and went. The last trilobites died out in a mass extinction 250 million years ago.

Trinucleus
450 million years ago

Angelina
490 million years ago

Kolihapeltis
400 million years ago

▲ Many different kinds of trilobites evolved and died out over millions of years.

309
Scientists know about long-gone extinct species from their fossils. These are remains of body parts such as the bones, teeth, horns, claws and shells of animals, and the bark, roots and leaves of plants, which have been preserved in rocks and turned to stone.

310
Studying millions of fossils of thousands of extinct species all around the world shows how different kinds of living things came and went long ago. This 'turnover' of species gives the average rate of extinction. For every one million species, one species would die out about once each year.

▲ Scientists have studied more than one million trilobite fossils.

▶ *Stegosaurus* was one of the longest-lasting dinosaur species. Its kind survived for over ten million years.

▼ Magnolias are flowering plants that have successfully evolved from 100 million years ago to today.

311
Fossil studies show the typical time for a species or genus to survive before going extinct. A mammal species lasted from one to two million years. For sea-living invertebrates (creatures without backbones) such as crabs, species survived between five and ten million years.

Why does it happen?

312 There are several reasons for extinction. Many extinctions are combinations of these reasons. We cannot know for sure why prehistoric species became extinct. But we can see the reasons for extinctions today. These may help us to understand what happened in the past.

313 One reason for extinction is competition. A species cannot get enough of its needs, such as food or living space, because other species need them too, and are better at getting them. These competing species may be newly evolved, or may have spread from afar.

314 A species can be forced to extinction by predators, parasites or diseases. Again, all of these could be new dangers as a result of evolution.

▼ In Australia, introduced farm animals such as sheep, and also wild rabbits, have been better than local species at gaining food.

▲ Australia's rock wallabies have suffered due to competition from sheep and goats.

315

Another cause is when conditions change rapidly. In the distant past there were many periods of natural global warming, when the world became hot and tropical, and then global cooling, when vast ice sheets covered huge areas. Some species could not evolve fast enough to survive the changing conditions.

▲ The giant ant is known from its 50 million-year-old fossils. It was big and fierce, so why did it die out?

316

Genes are chemical instructions inside living things. They determine how animals and plants grow, live and survive – and they have great effects on extinction. If there are very few members of a species, called a 'gene pool', there may not be enough gene variety for the species to evolve and adapt to new conditions.

▼ Interbreeding between species such as the coyote and grey wolf complicates saving the rare red wolf.

317

Another cause of extinction is when one species evolves to become so similar to another that the two species can interbreed. They produce 'halfway' offspring called hybrids. If hybrids become well adapted they may gradually take over, and the original species might disappear.

Grey wolf

Red wolf

Coyote

How do we know?

318 **How do we know if a species is extinct?** The more recent the extinction, the harder it is to say. How long should we wait before saying a species is extinct? It might be found living in a remote area years later.

319 **Wildlife experts at the IUCN** (International Union for Conservation of Nature) say that a species cannot be declared extinct until 50 years have passed with no real sightings of it, or evidence such as droppings or eggshells.

▲ Leadbeater's possums were restricted to a very small area, as land around was turned into farms.

320 **Sometimes, a species thought to be extinct 'comes back from the dead'.** Usually it has survived in an unexplored area. It is called a 'Lazarus species' after a man in the Bible who came to life again after he died.

321 **One 'Lazarus species' is the squirrel-like Leadbeater's possum of Australia.** It was thought to be extinct by the 1930s, but in 1965, a group was found living in highland forests in southeast Australia. Plant 'Lazarus species' include the jellyfish tree and Monte Diablo buckwheat.

322 Some people consider creatures such as the yeti (abominable snowman), bunyip and Bigfoot to be extinct. But most scientists would say that these creatures are only from tales and legends. There is no real scientific proof they ever lived, so they cannot be extinct.

323 Some species are 'extinct in the wild'. This means all surviving members are in zoos, wildlife parks or gardens. One example is the toromiro, a tree that disappeared from Easter Island in the Pacific. Experts saved some at Kew Gardens, London, and it is now being taken back to its original home.

▶ A toromiro flower. The toromiro tree once covered parts of Easter Island, but it was wiped out in the wild.

▲ The huge, hairy yeti of the Himalayas is well known in myths and stories, but no real evidence of its existance has been discovered.

▼ In 1987, only 22 Californian condors were left in the wild. All were captured for breeding and chicks were raised using 'condor parent' puppet gloves.

FAME AT LAST

You will need:
books about Australia
the Internet

Look in books or on the Internet for information about the state of Victoria in Australia. See if you can find the state's animal emblem or symbol, and a picture of it. That's Leadbeater's possum!

Not quite extinct

◀ Pterosaurs (pterodactyls) were flying reptiles that died out with the dinosaurs 65 million years ago.

324 **It's easy to decide if prehistoric species are extinct.** No one has seen living dinosaurs. Some myths and legends say they exist, but there's no scientific proof. So we assume all dinosaurs are extinct.

325 Some 'Lazarus species' lived millions of years ago in prehistoric times, but have been recently rediscovered. Fossils show that the coelacanth fish died out over 60 million years ago. In 1938 one was caught off southeast Africa, with more seen since.

▼ Coelacanth fish of today are not exactly the same species from millions of years ago, but very similar.

326 **Living species (such as the coelacanth) that are very similar to long-extinct ones are known as 'living fossils'.** They help us to understand how evolution works and how the original species may have become extinct.

327 When a particular species is known to be living, it is called 'extant' rather than 'extinct'. Other examples of extant 'living fossils' include Australia's Wollemi pine tree, the pig-like Chacoan peccary, and the shellfish known as the lampshell.

▲ The Chacoan peccary is similar to the giant Ice Age peccary that disappeared 10,000 years ago.

328 A tree 'living fossil' once thought to be extinct is the dawn redwood. It was known only from fossils dating back ten million years. Then in 1944, examples were found in China. The living species, *Metasequoia glyptostroboides*, is slightly different to the long-extinct species.

◀ Large copper butterflies are still found in mainland Europe, but habitats lost to farming mean they are rare.

▶ The dawn redwood, one of only three redwood species, is now planted in parks and gardens across the world.

329 A particular plant or creature may become extinct in one area but be extant in another. In Europe the large copper butterfly became extinct in Britain in the 1860s, but it still lives in many other places across the region.

Beliefs and ideas

330 **The way people view extinction has changed through the ages.** Scientists' thoughts can be very different to those of other people. Some people don't believe in extinction, perhaps due to religious ideas.

331 **In ancient times, people such as the Greek scientist–naturalist Aristotle (384–322 BC) believed that the natural world had never changed.** No new species evolved and no old ones became extinct.

332 **As people began to study fossils, they realized that they were from living things that were no longer around.** Some experts said these plants and animals survived somewhere remote and undiscovered. Others began to suggest that extinction really did happen.

333 **Fossil expert Georges Cuvier (1769–1832) was one of the first scientists to say that there probably were extinctions.** Due to his religious beliefs, he explained them as happening in the Great Floods described in the Bible.

▼ Baron Georges Cuvier admitted that the fossil elephants he studied had become extinct.

▲ By altering the malaria-carrying mosquito's genes, scientists may be able to wipe out the disease malaria.

▼ In South America, Darwin studied fossils of the giant armadillo-like *Glyptodon* and wondered why it no longer survived.

335 Modern views continue to change about extinction. Scientists can now identify separate species by studying their genes, rather than what they look like or how they breed. What was thought to be one species could, with genetic information, be two or more. For endangered plants and animals, it might not be one species threatened with extinction, but several.

334 In 1859, extinction became an important topic. Naturalist Charles Darwin described the theory of evolution in his book *On the Origin of Species by Means of Natural Selection*. In it Darwin explained the idea of 'survival of the fittest', and how new species evolved while other species less equipped to deal with their environment died out.

▶ A scene from the 2009 movie *Creation*. Darwin's ideas about evolution shaped modern scientific views on extinction.

Long, long ago

336 The history of life on Earth dates back over three billion years, and extinction has been happening since then. Millions of plants and animals have died out over this time, called the geological timescale.

337 Fossil evidence shows that even 500 million years ago, there was an enormous variety of life with many species becoming extinct. The idea that long ago there were just a few species, which gradually increased through to today, with new ones evolving but very few dying out, is not accurate.

▼ Spiny sharks such as *Acanthodes* flourished in Devonian times but gradually died out.

Acanthodes fossil

MILLIONS OF YEARS AGO	PERIOD	ERA
2.0 / 23	QUATERNARY NEOGENE	CENOZOIC ERA
	PALEOGENE	
65		
	CRETACEOUS	MESOZOIC ERA
145	JURASSIC	
199	TRIASSIC	
251	PERMIAN	PALEOZOIC ERA
299		
	CARBONIFEROUS	
359	DEVONIAN	
416	SILURIAN	
443	ORDOVICIAN	
488	CAMBRIAN	
540		

▲ The geological timescale spans the history of the Earth. This vast amount of time is broken down into eras, and then into time periods. By studying fossils from different periods we can see how abundant life was through prehistory.

338

As we find more fossils, the gaps or 'missing links' in the history of life are filled, and we identify more and more extinctions. Fossils show how whole groups of prehistoric living things started, spread and became common, then faded away. For example, there are many kinds of reptiles alive today, such as crocodiles, snakes, lizards and turtles. But other reptiles, such as dinosaurs, pterosaurs and ichthyosaurs, are long extinct.

Glossopteris fossil

▲ *Glossopteris* or Gondwana tree once covered huge areas, but disappeared.

QUIZ

Match these extinct animals with their descriptions:
1. Pterosaur 2. Ichthyosaur 3. Early amphibian
A. Dolphin-shaped sea reptile
B. Four-legged swamp-dweller with a fishy tail C. Flying creature with long, thin jaws and claws on its wings and feet

Answers:
1C 2A 3B

▼ Ichthyosaurs became extinct with the dinosaurs, 65 million years ago.

Ichthyosaur fossil

339

Fossils also reveal that during some time periods, life was very varied, with lots of new species appearing and others dying out. At other times, plants and animals were less numerous and varied, with fewer new species evolving and lower numbers of extinctions.

▼ *Acanthostega* was one of the first four-legged land creatures.

Acanthostega fossil

◀ The extinct fish *Tiktaalik* shows a link between fish and land animals.

Tiktaalik fossil

Mass extinctions

340 At times in the Earth's history there have been mass extinctions, also called extinction events. Huge numbers of living things died out in a short time, usually less than a few thousand years. In some cases over half of all animals and plants disappeared.

ORDOVICIAN-SILURIAN
450–443 million years ago

Endoceras:
A type of mollusc

CAMBRIAN-ORDOVICIAN
488 million years ago

Pikaia:
An eel-like creature with a rod-like spinal column

▶ These are just a few of the millions of animals and plants that died out during mass extinctions.

341 The Cambrian–Ordovician mass extinction was 488 million years ago. It marked the change from the time span called the Cambrian Period to the next one, the Ordovician Period. Among the victims were many kinds of trilobites and lampshells, a kind of shellfish.

342 The Ordovician–Silurian mass extinction happened 450–443 million years ago, in two bursts. All life was in the sea at that time. Many types of shellfish, echinoderms (starfish, sea urchins and relatives) and corals died out.

▶ Mass extinctions show as dips in the variety of living things throughout prehistoric time.

Cambrian–Ordovician

Ordovician–Silurian

600　　　　　500　　　　　400　　　Time (million years ago)

CRETACEOUS–TERTIARY
65 million years ago

Triceratops:
One of the last dinosaurs

343 The Late Devonian mass extinction included several bursts 365–359 million years ago. Corals, trilobites and several groups of fish disappeared. It was the end of the 'Age of Fishes'.

LATE DEVONIAN
365–359 million years ago

TRIASSIC–JURASSIC
200 million years ago

Placodus:
A marine reptile

Dunkleosteus:
An armoured fish

344 The Triassic–Jurassic mass extinction occurred 200 million years ago. The main groups affected included many sea creatures, amphibians, and certain types of reptiles, including some early dinosaurs.

345 The Cretaceous–Tertiary mass extinction, 65 million years ago, is the most famous. It saw the extinction of the dinosaurs, as well as many other animals and plants. More than two-thirds of all species died out. The cause may have been a meteorite that smashed into Earth, setting off earthquakes, tsunamis and volcanoes, and causing rapid climate change.

Late Devonian

Triassic–Jurassic

Cretaceous–Tertiary

Number of families

800

0

200

100

0

The biggest of all

346
The most massive of all mass extinctions was the Permian-Triassic or end-of Permian event, 251 million years ago. Also known as the 'Great Dying' it saw vast losses with more than four-fifths of all Earth's species wiped out.

347
The 'Great Dying' was probably caused by the same combination of reasons as several other mass extinctions. These included volcanic eruptions, earthquakes and tsunamis. They were probably set off by the continents drifting into new positions, with accompanying changes in sea levels, ocean currents, wind patterns, rainfall and temperature.

▶ At the end of the Permian Period, the world was rocked by a series of great changes that killed off most kinds of life on Earth.

348
The changes that probably caused mass extinctions were very complicated because of the way species depend on each other. If a particular plant could not cope with the changes and died out, then the animals that fed on it were also affected, as were the predators that fed on them. The balance of nature was upset and extinctions followed.

Crinoids

Acanthodian fish

Placoderms

349 **Mass extinctions upset some habitats more than others.** In many of these events, including the Permian-Triassic one, most losses were marine life. Especially affected were tiny sea plants and creatures that formed the floating 'soup' of life known as plankton.

Diictodon

Lystrosaurus

Gorgonops

350 **Mass extinctions were not total disasters.** Afterwards, fewer species meant less competition. So there were chances and opportunities for a surge of evolution and new species. Just 20 million years after the Permian-Triassic 'Great Dying', the first dinosaurs were prowling the land while early pterosaurs flapped through the skies.

Corals

Trilobites

153

Ages of ice

351 Over the past few million years there have been several extinctions linked to more than a dozen ice ages. The first of these started around 2.6 million years ago and the last one faded just 15,000–10,000 years ago. These cold times are called glaciations, and the warmer periods between – like the one today – are interglacials.

352 An example of an extinct ice age species is the sabre-tooth cat *Smilodon*. There were perhaps five species of *Smilodon* starting around 2.5 million years ago. The last one, dying out only 10,000 years ago, was *Smilodon fatalis*.

▲ Last of the ice age sabre-tooth cats, *Smilodon* lived in the Americas and was as big as the largest big cat of today, the Siberian tiger.

353 Hundreds of other ice age animals have died out in the past 25,000 years. They include the woolly rhino, woolly mammoth, cave bear, dire wolf, and various kinds of horses, deer, camels, llamas, beavers, ground sloths, and even mice and rats.

356 The second reason is the spread of humans. As the climate warmed, ice sheets and glaciers melted, and people moved north into new areas. Big animals such as mammoths were hunted for food, as shown in Stone Age cave paintings. Others, such as cave bears, were killed because they were dangerous.

354 Many of these large animals disappeared during a fairly short time period of 15,000–10,000 years ago. This happened especially across northern lands in North America, Europe and Asia. What was the cause of such widespread losses?

355 Two main reasons have been suggested for the recent ice age extinctions. One is rapid natural climate change. As the weather warmed up, some big animals could not evolve fast enough or travel to cooler areas. The woolly mammoth and woolly rhino, for example, may have overheated.

▼ Low sea levels during ice ages allowed people to spread from eastern Asia to North America.

SIBERIA

ARCTIC OCEAN

NORTH AMERICA

Alaska

PACIFIC OCEAN

▶ Stone Age people probably trapped and killed mammoths, which would have provided them with food for weeks.

Keeping a record

357 In ancient times, people travelled little and did not record details of nature, so extinctions were hard to identify. From the 1500s, people began to explore the world, study living things and discover new species. They then hunted, shot, ate or collected them – some to extinction.

▲ People exploring remote areas brought back tales of fanciful beasts – perhaps the result of several real creatures that explorers mixed up.

358 Spectacular examples of historical extinction are the elephant birds of Madagascar. There were several species of these giant, flightless birds, similar to ostriches but larger. The biggest stood 3 metres tall and weighed more than 450 kilograms.

359 All elephant birds were extinct by the 1500s. People not only hunted them, but also collected and cooked their huge eggs, more than 35 centimetres in length.

▼ Elephant birds evolved on the island of Madagascar with no big predators to threaten them – until humans arrived.

Steller's sea cow was 8 metres long

Great auks once numbered millions

Bluebuck lived in small herds

▲ Extinctions of large creatures continued through recent centuries.

360 There is a long list of other animal species that went extinct even before 1900. They include the tall New Zealand ground birds called moas (by 1500), the huge European cow known as the auroch (probably 1630s), the North Pacific Steller's sea cow (1760s), the Southern African bluebuck antelope (around 1800) and the Atlantic penguin-like great auk (1850s).

The huge moa of New Zealand was 4 metres tall. It was hunted by the enormous Haast's eagle, the biggest known eagle, which became extinct by 1400.

361 Many plants are also recorded as going extinct during this time. They include the Rio myrtle tree from South America (about 1820s), the string tree from the Atlantic island of St Helena (1860s) and the Indian kerala tree (1880s).

◀ St Helena ebony is a shrub that is being rescued from the brink of extinction.

Gathering pace

362 Over the last 100 years, the rate of extinction has speeded up greatly. More kinds of living things are disappearing than ever before. This is due mainly to human activity such as cutting down forests, habitat loss as natural areas are changed for farmland and houses, hunting, collecting rare species, and releasing chemicals into the environment.

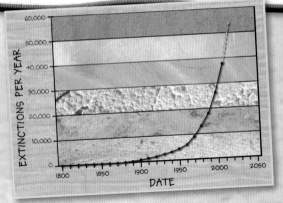

▲ The estimated extinction rate is rocketing as we find out about more threatened species every year.

▶ The spectacled bear of South America's Andes Mountains faces many threats, including the logging of its forest home.

363 One of the first extinctions to receive lots of publicity around the world was the Caribbean monk seal in the 1950s. It was hunted for its oil and meat, and to stop it eating the fish that people wanted to catch. From 2003, expeditions tried to find it again but gave up after five years.

▲ The last confirmed sightings of Caribbean monk seals were southeast of the island of Jamaica in 1952.

Thylacine

364 Other animal extinctions of the last 100 years include the thylacine and the Japanese sea lion. The last thylacine died of neglect in a zoo in Hobart, Tasmania in 1936, while the last Japanese sea lion was seen in 1974. Many plant species have also died out in the last 100 years, including the Cuban holly (1950s), the cry violet or cry pansy in France (1950s) and the woolly begonia of Malaysia (1960s).

365 With each passing year scientists explore, identify and record more living species in more detail than ever before. As we study and list all of these new plants and animals, we have a greater chance of discovering when one goes extinct.

▼ The Bosavi silky cuscus is a rarity — a new species discovered in Papua New Guinea.

FIND THAT SEAL!

You will need:
paper   pens

Imagine you are on an expedition to search for the Caribbean monk seal. Make a list of the equipment you would need. Binoculars, cameras, sketch pad, sound recorder... You need evidence, so don't forget specimen bottles for some of the seal's hair, or its urine or droppings!

Too many to disappear

366 The passenger pigeon was once extremely common. Flocks of millions flew around North America, darkening the skies as they passed. Before Europeans arrived in North America, native people caught the pigeons for their meat and feathers. This was on a small scale and happened for centuries without affecting the overall number of birds.

367 With the arrival of Europeans, especially from about 1700, came many changes. The new settlers altered the land from natural habitats to farms, roads and towns. Habitat loss soon gathered pace, and people also began to catch the pigeons for a cheap supply of food.

▼ Today, birds such as these city starlings seem too numerous to vanish. But we cannot be sure how they will fare in the future.

► Passenger pigeons became big business, with hunters shooting and trappers netting the birds to sell their meat in cities.

▲ Famous hunter, naturalist and artist John James Audobon painted passenger pigeons. He once said one flock was 'still passing in undiminished numbers... for three days'.

368 By the 1850s, the hunters and trappers noticed that passenger pigeon numbers had started to fall. But the killing continued. Some people tried to raise the pigeons in captivity, but the birds could only breed and thrive in very large flocks. Kept in small groups, they did not eat well or breed. They may have also suffered from a bird illness called Newcastle disease.

369 By 1900, the passenger pigeon had just about disappeared in the wild. The last one in captivity, Martha, died in Cincinnati Zoo, Ohio, USA in 1914. With her went one of the most numerous birds that ever existed.

I DON'T BELIEVE IT!

Martha, the last passenger pigeon, was named after Martha Washington, wife of the first US president George Washington. There are several statues and memorials to Martha (the pigeon), including one at Cincinnati Zoo.

▲ Passenger pigeons did not survive well in captivity. When the last one died in 1914, it was mounted or 'stuffed' at the Smithsonian Institute.

Island extinctions

Hawaii

▼ Tiny islands in vast oceans around the world are 'hotbeds' of extinctions.

CUBA

Galapagos Islands

Cuban solenodon – this shrew-like creature has not been seen since 1999

Hawaiian black mamo – gone by the 1920s

PACIFIC OCEAN

Galapagos damselfish – became extinct during the 1980s

SOUTHERN ATLANTIC OCEAN

370 In the past few centuries, more than two-thirds of living things becoming extinct have lived on islands. Islands can support only small numbers of a particular species, so there is a higher risk of dying out. Each island also has its own particular conditions, to which species adapt over thousands of years. If conditions change, for example, when people arrive, the local wild species may be threatened.

371 Island plants and animals are also at great risk from introduced species – those brought by people. These introduced species include sheep, goats, cows, foxes, stoats, mice, rats, cats and dogs. They start to compete with the local species for food, or prey on them, or steal their nest sites, or give them diseases – or all of these.

PACIFIC OCEAN

MAURITIUS

AUSTRALIA

Lesser bilby – not seen on the island continent of Australia since the 1950s

INDIAN OCEAN

Mauritius dodo – disappeared by the 1690s

THE DODO LIVES AGAIN!

You will need:
sheet of card   scissors   coloured pens
sticky tape   elastic

Cut out a face mask in the shape of a dodo's head and beak and colour it as shown (left). Find out from books or the Internet about the noises a dodo made. Now you can try to bring the dodo back to life!

372 Perhaps the most famous example of any extinct animal is the dodo. This flightless, turkey-sized bird lived on Mauritius in the Indian Ocean, ate fruit and nested on the ground. It had no natural predators or enemies. Then people arrived with animals that hunted it, its eggs and its chicks. By 1700, the dodo was gone, leading to the saying 'dead as a dodo'.

373 At least 50 bird species from the Hawaiian Islands are extinct. This affected other wildlife. Some of the birds fed on nectar and carried pollen so that flowers could breed. Others ate fruits and spread the seeds in their droppings. Without the birds, some of these plants become extinct. When one species disappears, then another that depends on it dies out, it is known as co-extinction.

What's happening today?

374 In the natural world today, extinction rates are shooting up due to a huge variety of causes. Scientists call this another time of mass extinction.

375 The main cause of today's extinctions is habitat loss and degradation (changing natural habitats for the worse). The number of people in the world is rising fast and they need land for their houses, farms, factories, roads and leisure, leaving less wild areas.

▲ Acid rain from polluting gases taken up by clouds has devastated large areas of forest.

◀ Logging and other forms of deforestation are major threats in tropical areas.

376 Other causes include pollution and hunting for food or trophies. There is also the collecting of species for displays, introduced species, and diseases that spread from domestic animals and farm plants to wild species. As the early signs of global warming and climate change become more marked, these will also have huge effects on habitats and push species towards extinction.

▲ The baiji is probably now extinct. Some people hope it survives in backwaters of the Yangtze and nearby rivers. There are rare sightings, but for the time being, no proof.

377 In 2007, a search in China failed to find any baijis, or Yangtze river dolphins. This species was threatened for many reasons, including dams built across its rivers, pollution, hunting and the overfishing of its natural prey.

▼ Now extinct, golden toads were probably victims of global warming and increased human activity in their natural habitats.

On the brink

378 Every year, wildlife experts make lists of animals and plants that are threatened with extinction. These are known as the IUCN 'Red Lists', and every year, they grow longer.

▶ Symbols indicate if a species is threatened or not, ranging from LC meaning Least Concern, to EX meaning Extinct.

QUIZ

Which of these amphibians is threatened with extinction?
1. Lungless Mexican salamander
2. South African ghost frog
3. Betic midwife toad
4. Chinese giant salamander
5. Darwin frog

Answer:
All of them, plus thousands of others

379 One of the most endangered groups of animals is the rhinos. There are only five rhino species and all are in huge trouble. The black, Javan and Sumatran rhinos are listed as 'critically endangered'. They will become extinct in 20–50 years unless massive efforts are made to save them.

▼ All rhinos need action to save them. Most numerous is the white rhino, with less than 20,000.

Sumatran rhino

White rhino

Javan rhino

Black rhino

380

A larger group, with many species at risk of extinction, is the amphibians. More than half of the 6000-plus species are threatened. A terrible problem is the new fungus infection called chytrid disease. Recent amphibian extinctions include the gastric-brooding frog of Australia, which swallowed its eggs so the tadpoles could grow in its stomach. It died out in the 1980s.

▲ Baby gastric-brooding frogs emerged from their mother's mouth. Many other species of frogs, toads and newts are also under threat.

381

You cannot get closer to extinction than only one remaining individual. The café marron bush grew on the island of Rodrigues in the Indian Ocean, but finally only one bush was left. Scientists at Kew Gardens, London took cuttings from it in the 1980s and grew them into bushes. Now some are being taken back to Rodrigues.

▲ The world's largest flower, rafflesia, is now extremely rare.

Indian rhino

382

Coral reefs are among the world's richest places for wildlife. But these whole habitats may become extinct in the next 100–200 years. They are in great danger from threats such as global warming, pollution, water cloudiness and acidity upsetting the delicate natural balance between their species.

► Due to global warming, coral reefs may become 'bleached' and die.

Saved just in time

383 To save an almost extinct species takes time, effort and money. This means studying it and its habitat, its contact with other species and finding out how many are left. Scientists assess its needs through field studies – in the wild – and also captive studies. They establish what it eats, where it nests or which soil it likes, so that places can be put aside.

Female

Male

▲ Through a huge conservation effort, the numbers of ladybird spiders in Great Britain have risen.

384 Rescuing a threatened animal or plant from extinction also means saving its habitat. Without somewhere natural and safe to live, the species cannot thrive in the wild. Otherwise, even if it is saved, it will always be limited to a park, zoo or similar place, and be extinct in the wild.

▼ In North America, movements of very rare black-footed ferrets are studied by radio transmitter collars.

385

It's less use people coming to an area from far away, and trying to save a species, than local people getting involved. The locals need to have input into the rescue effort. Through ecotourism, visitors can see rare wildlife without damaging it or the habitat and pay money, which is put towards conservation efforts.

SAVE OUR SPIDER

You will need:
large sheet of paper
coloured pens

Spiders may not be everyone's favourite animal, but they deserve saving as much as other species. Find out about the ladybird spider, which is almost extinct in Britain. Make a colourful poster telling people why it should not be allowed to die out.

◀ Elephant safaris allow paying tourists to get close to rare rhinos without disturbing them too much.

386

Saving one 'flagship' or 'headline' species from extinction can help to save whole habitats. Such species usually appeal to the public because they are big and powerful, like tigers and mountain gorillas, or cute and fluffy, like giant pandas and golden lion tamarins.

▼ Setting up wildlife parks and nature reserves helps not only the headline species, such as these gorillas, but all the plants and animals living there.

169

Should we care?

387 **Why should we care if a species goes extinct?** Especially if it is some small bug in a remote forest, or a worm on the seabed. Does it really matter or affect us in any way?

388 **Many people think that all animals and plants have a right to be here on Earth.** We should not destroy nature for little reason. If we let species die out, it shows we do not care for our surroundings and the natural world. These types of reasons are known as moral and ethical arguments.

389 **There are medical reasons for saving species.** Researchers may discover that a particular type of plant or animal is the source of a new wonder drug to cure illness. If it had gone extinct, we would never know this. Other species can be used for medical research into diseases such as cancers.

390 **Scientific reasons to prevent species dying out are also important.** Extinction reduces biodiversity, which is the variety of living things necessary for the balance of nature. The genes in certain animals or plants could be used in GM, genetic modification, perhaps to improve our farm crops and make our farm animals healthier.

391 **There are also traditional and cultural reasons for caring about extinction.** Some endangered species are important to ethnic groups and tribes for their history, ceremonies, myths and special foods. People should not come to an area from afar with new ways of living and cause habitat loss, introduce new animals, plants and diseases and kill off local species.

▲ The Florida panther is an extremely rare subspecies of cougar, or mountain lion. If it dies out, there will still be other cougars elsewhere. So would its disappearance matter?

Gone forever?

392 People once thought that extinction is forever, but future science may change this view. The idea of bringing extinct animals or plants back to life can be seen through films such as *Jurassic Park*. Scientists use a species' eggs, its genes or its genetic material such as DNA (de-oxyribonucleic acid).

▲ In the *Jurassic Park* stories, dinosaurs were recreated from their preserved genes and hatched in egg incubators.

▼ Why the Pyrenean ibex died out is unclear, but it may have been the result of infectious diseases.

393 In 2009, a baby Pyrenean ibex, a subspecies of the goat-like Spanish ibex, was born. Its mother was a goat but its genes came from one of the last Pyrenean ibexes, which had died out by 2000. The young ibex was a genetic copy. It died after birth, but it showed what might be possible in future.

QUIZ

Put these species in order of when they became extinct, from longest ago to most recent.
1. Quagga
2. Dodo
3. Neanderthal humans
4. Baiji (Yangtze river dolphin)
5. Woolly mammoth

Answers:
3. About 30,000 years ago
5. Around 10,000 years ago
2. By 1700 1. 1883 4. By 2007 (probably)

394

To revive extinct species, there are many problems to solve in genetic engineering, altering DNA, cloning and similar methods. However scientists are taking samples of DNA and other material from all kinds of sources, such as frozen mammoths, dodo bones, the dead seeds of extinct plants, and even long-gone humans, to carry out experiments and see what can be done.

▲ The Barbary lion of North Africa was thought to be extinct from the 1920s, but genetic tests have revealed several living in zoos.

▼ The Quagga Project selects and breeds the most quagga-like zebras over many generations.

395

The quagga, which went extinct in 1883, was a subspecies of the plains zebra of southern Africa. It had zebra stripes on its front half but was plain brown at the rear. The Quagga Project aims to 'breed back' quaggas. This is done by choosing plains zebras that look most like quaggas, and allowing them to mate. Gradually, after several generations, the young of plains zebras should look more and more like quaggas.

Looking to the future

396 In the future, living things will continue to go extinct, with or without human meddling — because that is the nature of life and how it evolves. The damage we are doing to the world, especially with habitat loss and climate change, means that the rate of extinction will only increase.

Ardipithecus ramidus
Extinct: 4.5 million years ago

Australopithecus afarensis
Extinct: 3.5 million years ago

Homo ergaster
Extinct: 1.9 million years ago

Homo erectus
Extinct: 1.7 million years ago

397 What about our own kind, human beings? Over the past four million years there have probably been more than 20 different species of humans and their close cousins on Earth. Only one is left now – ourselves, modern humans, known as *Homo sapiens*. All others have gone extinct.

▲ There have been many different species of human throughout history. Despite advances such as stone tools and controlling fire, they all became extinct.

398 A recent human extinction is the Neanderthal people, *Homo neanderthalensis*. They lived about 250,000 years ago across northern Europe and Asia. As modern humans spread from Africa into Europe and Asia, Neanderthals died out. Whether modern people killed them, or were better at finding food and shelter, is not clear.

Recent surveys indicate that 1 in 8 bird species are at risk of extinction, and within 100 years this could rise to 1 in 4. And birds are a lot less threatened than many other animal groups.

399 Surviving even later than the Neanderthals, but still becoming extinct, were the 'hobbit people' on the island of Flores, Southeast Asia. Known as *Homo floresiensis*, they were only about one metre tall. They may have survived until less than 15,000 years ago.

▶ The remains of *Homo floresiensis* were discovered in 2003. It may be a new species of extinct human.

Homo floresiensis Extinct: 15,000 years ago

Homo heidelbergensis Extinct: 600,000 years ago

Homo neanderthalensis Extinct: 100,000 years ago

400 In the distant future, will humans become extinct? Our knowledge of the natural world, and the harm we are doing it, suggests that our species will not last forever. But humans have shown great skill at surviving all kinds of problems, and are likely to carry on for a very long time yet.

▶ Can modern humans use their wit and intelligence to survive – whilst also saving wild species?

Homo sapiens Still alive today

175

Animals in peril

401 **Around the world, wild animals, plants and the places they live in are disappearing fast.** From the creatures of the rainforests to the animals that live in mountains, deserts, polar lands, and even in the oceans, countless numbers are under threat. Some animals have become so rare, they will die out forever. The main problem is that people are causing huge amounts of damage to the natural world. It is up to us to change our ways and save animals in danger.

▶ The biggest cat in the Americas, the jaguar is threatened by loss of its habitat. It is also shot or trapped by people in case it attacks their farm animals, their pets — or themselves.

Gone long ago

402 In one sense, animals and plants have always been under threat. It's part of nature's 'struggle for existence'. Creatures must find food, shelter and other needs, and avoid predators and dangers. This has been happening for millions of years, as old types of living things died out, or became extinct, and new ones took over.

Saltasaurus

403 About 65 million years ago, the dinosaurs died out, along with many other animals and plants. This was a mass extinction, but it had nothing to do with people, because there were no humans then. Scientists are not sure why it happened, but the causes were natural. A huge asteroid may have smashed into the Earth. There have been many mass extinctions in the Earth's long history.

▲ The huge *Saltasaurus*, 12 metres long and weighing 8 tonnes, was one of the last dinosaurs. About 65 million years ago, it may have watched as a massive meteorite was about to smash into the Earth and cause the death of millions of animals and plants.

I DON'T BELIEVE IT!

More than 99 out of 100 kinds of animals that ever lived are now extinct — died out and gone for ever.

Pteranodon

404 Now there are humans on Earth, animals are becoming extinct at a faster rate than before. Woolly mammoths died out within the past 10,000 years. This may have been partly due to the end of the Ice Age, since they could not cope with warmer weather. However, being hunted by ancient people did not help.

Huge meteorite or asteroid

405 Many other large creatures have died out in the past few thousand years. These include cave bears, woolly rhinos, dire wolves and giant deer. Some of these extinctions happened as people spread around the world.

Herd of *Edmontosaurus*

406 As the centuries passed, from ancient history to medieval times, more animals came under threat. The auroch was a huge wild cow, from which today's farm cattle were bred. It was hunted by people until it disappeared. The last auroch died in 1627, in a Polish forest.

◄ Woolly rhinos were well adapted to the cold with their long coats. Perhaps they could not cope as the Ice Age faded and the world warmed up. They too became extinct.

179

Too late to save

407 **In the last few hundred years, many kinds of animals have become endangered, and dozens have died out.** They include fish, frogs, snakes, birds and mammals. Studying why these extinctions happened can help to save today's endangered animals.

408 **Being very common is no safeguard against human threats.** Five hundred years ago there were perhaps 5000 million passenger pigeons. They were shot and trapped by people for their meat, and their natural habitats were taken over by crops and farm animals. The last passenger pigeon, 'Martha', died in Cincinnati Zoo in 1914.

409 **A creature that went from discovery to extinction in less than 30 years was Steller's sea cow.** It was a huge, 3-tonne cousin of the manatee and dugong, and lived in the Arctic region. It was first described by scientists in 1741. So many were killed in a short space of time, that Steller's sea cow had died out by 1768.

▶ The dodo has become a world symbol of extinction. Only a few bones, feathers and bits of skin remain.

▲ Steller's sea cow was 8 metres long and almost as heavy as an elephant. However size was no protection, as its herds were slaughtered by sailors for meat, blubber and hides.

411 The dodo, a turkey-sized bird with tiny wings that could not fly, was found on the island of Mauritius in the Indian Ocean. Sailors that stopped at the island captured dodos as fresh food. So many were killed that all dodos were extinct by 1700. This has led to the saying 'as dead as a dodo'.

▼ Every 7 September, Australia holds National Threatened Species Day. The day is in memory of the last thylacine that died on this date in 1936 at Hobart Zoo, in the state of Tasmania.

410 Many animals have become endangered, and died out forever. They include the blue antelope of Southern Africa (around 1800), the flightless seabird known as the great auk (1850s), the dog-like marsupial (pouched mammal) known as the thylacine or Tasmanian tiger (1936), and the Caribbean monk seal (1950s). The list is very long, and very sad.

How we know

412 **How do we know which animals are endangered and need our help?** Explorers and travellers bring back stories of rare and strange creatures. Sometimes they add bits to their tales to make them more exciting. Scientific studies and surveys are needed to find out which creatures are in trouble, and how serious the threats are.

▼ This lion, put to sleep briefly by a tranquillizer dart, is being tracked by its radio collar. Each lion has its own pattern of whisker spots, like a fingerprint, to help identify it.

▼ Rangers guard incredibly rare mountain gorillas, which soon get used to having them around. The rangers become well acquainted with the habits of the gorillas, which helps scientists carry out important research.

413 Firing a dart containing a knock-out chemical makes a creature, such as a lion, sleep for a short time. Scientists then work fast to take blood samples, check for diseases, measure and weigh, and gather other useful information, before the animal wakes up.

414 Scientists need to know more than just how many individual animals are left in an endangered species. They try to find out the animals' ages, what they eat, how often they breed, how they move about or migrate, and how long they live. This all helps to build up knowledge of the species, and work out the best ways to take action.

▼ Aerial films and photographs can be studied to count big animals such as elephants, estimate their age and work out if they are male or female.

415 Big animals in open habitats, such as elephants on the African savanna (grassland), are surveyed from the air. Planes, helicopters and even balloons carry people who count the herds and take photographs.

416 It is extremely helpful to capture, tag and release animals. Rare birds such as albatrosses are carefully caught in nets, and small rings are put on their legs. This helps scientists to identify each albatross every time it is seen. Tags in the ears of rhinos can work in the same way.

I DON'T BELIEVE IT!

When studying an endangered animal, one of the best things to have is — its poo! Droppings or dung contain much information about what a creature eats, how healthy it is, and any diseases it may have.

417 Some animals are big enough to attach a radio beacon to, which sends signals up to a satellite. Whales, sea turtles, seals and other sea creatures can be tracked as they swim across the vast oceans.

How endangered?

418 We might suspect an animal is at risk, but how serious is the threat? The scientific organization called the IUCN, World Conservation Union, produces a 'Red List' of threatened species of animals and plants. Each species is given a two-letter description to show its plight.

▲ The leafy sea dragon is threatened as it is caught by exotic fish collectors. It is also killed, dried and powdered for the traditional medicine trade.

419 NT is Near Threatened. A species could be in trouble soon, but not quite yet. An example is the leafy sea dragon, a type of fish, whose flaps of skin make it look like swaying seaweed.

420 VU is Vulnerable. The species is already under threat, and help is needed over the coming years. An example is the northern fur seal, of the northern Pacific region.

◄ The northern fur seal was killed in large numbers for its thick, soft, warm fur, once used for coats.

► Cheetahs once lived across most of Africa and the Middle East, and were even partly tamed and kept as pets by royalty. They may disappear before long.

421
EN is Endangered. The species faces big problems and the risk of extinction over the coming years is high. An example is the cheetah, the fastest runner on Earth.

422
CR is Critically Endangered. This is the most serious group. Unless there is a huge conservation effort, extinction is just around the corner. An example is the vaquita, the smallest kind of porpoise, from the northern Gulf of California.

▲ Polluted water, drilling for oil and gas, and being caught in fishing nets are all deadly dangers for the 1.5-metre-long vaquita.

▼ Hawaiian crows are only found in captivity. Attempts to breed and release them have so far failed.

423
EW is Extinct in the Wild. The species has disappeared in nature, although there may be a few surviving in zoos and wildlife parks. An example is the Hawaiian crow. The last two wild birds disappeared in 2002, although some live in cages. EX is Extinct, or gone forever. Usually this means the animal has not been seen for 50 years.

MATCH UP

Can you place these threatened creatures in their correct animal groups?

A. Whale shark
B. Spix macaw
C. Vaquita
D. Caiman
E. Olm

1. Bird
2. Fish
3. Amphibian
4. Mammal
5. Reptile

Answers:
A2 B1 C4 D5 E3

185

On the critical list

424 **The most threatened animals in the world are CR, Critically Endangered.** One of the most famous CR mammals is the mountain gorilla. There are just a few hundred left in the high peaks of Central Africa. They suffer from loss of their natural habitat, being killed for meat and trophies, and from catching human diseases.

▲ Smallest of the rhinos, at about 700 kilograms, the Sumatran rhino is poached for its horns. These are powdered for use in traditional so-called 'medicines'.

425 **The most threatened group of big mammals is the rhinos.** Of the five species, three are CR – the Javan and Sumatran rhinos of Southeast Asia, and the black rhino of Africa. The Indian rhino is endangered, EN. They all suffer from loss of natural living areas and being killed for their horns.

▼ Although more numerous than their mountain cousins, lowland gorillas face the same threats – loss of habitat and poaching being the two most dangerous.

MAKE A RHINO NOSE

You will need:
Large sheet of card   Sticky tape

A rhino's nose horn may be more than one metre long! Make your own by rolling some card into a cone shape and taping it firmly. Hold the 'horn' angled up from your own nose. How do rhinos see where they are going?

426 The kouprey or Cambodian forest ox is another critical mammal. It has big horns and weighs more than one tonne, but there are probably fewer than 250 left in Southeast Asia. Apart from losing its natural habitat, the kouprey is hunted by local people and it catches diseases from farm cattle. It is also killed for food by soldiers who fight for local warlords and hide in the forest.

▲ The kouprey grazes on grasses by night and hides in the thick forest during the day.

▼ Right whales are slow swimmers and stay near the surface, which made them easy targets for whalers.

427 The northern right whale has never recovered from being slaughtered during the mass killing of whales in the last century. There are now probably less than 600 left. These whales breed so slowly that they may never increase in numbers.

428 Apart from big, well-known mammals, many other smaller mammal species are on the critical list. They include the hispid hare (Assam rabbit) and dwarf blue sheep of the Himalaya Mountains, and the northern hairy-nosed wombat of northeast Australia.

187

All kinds under threat

▲ The young Bermuda petrel stays at sea for about five years before it comes back to land to breed.

429 Mammals such as pandas, whales and tigers are not the only endangered animals — there are many other threatened species from all animal groups. Among the birds is the Bermuda petrel, the national seabird of the island of Bermuda. Only about 250 survive and the islanders are making a huge conservation effort to help them.

430 A critical reptile is the Batagur baska (river turtle or terrapin) of India and Southeast Asia. One reason for its rarity was that people collected its eggs, especially in Cambodia, to give as presents to the king. King Norodom Sihamoni of Cambodia has now given orders to protect the baska.

▼ The batagur 'royal turtle' grows to more than one metre long and 30 kilograms in weight. It eats all kinds of foods, from plants to fish and crabs.

431 An endangered amphibian is Hamilton's frog of New Zealand. It is perhaps the rarest frog in the world. Hamilton's frog does not croak, does not have webbed feet, and hatches from its egg not as a tadpole, but as a fully formed froglet.

▲ Hamilton's frog is less than 5 cm long. There may be as few as 300 left in the wild.

▼ The Devil's Hole pupfish is one of several very rare fish, each found in one small pool.

432 A fish that is vulnerable (VU) is the Devil's Hole pupfish. It lives naturally in just one warm pool, Devil's Hole, in a limestone cave in the desert near Death Valley, USA. There are usually around 200–400 pupfish there, but after problems with floods and droughts, the number by 2006 was less than 50.

433 One of the rarest insects is the Queen Alexandra's birdwing butterfly. It lives in a small area on the island of Papua New Guinea. In 1950, a nearby volcano erupted and destroyed much of the butterfly's forest habitat, so it is now endangered (EN).

Male

▶ Like many tropical butterflies, the female and male Queen Alexandra's birdwing look quite different from each other.

Female

I DON'T BELIEVE IT!

The Bermuda petrel was thought to be extinct for over 300 years until a breeding group was discovered on some coastal rocks in 1951.

189

The greatest threat

434 Endangered animals face dozens of different threats, but the greatest problem for most of them is habitat loss. This means the wild places or natural habitats where they live are being changed or destroyed, so animals, plants and other wildlife can no longer survive there.

435 Habitat loss is not a new threat – it has been happening for thousands of years. Across much of Europe, farmland for crops and livestock gradually replaced once-great woods and forests. This meant the disappearance from Britain of forest animals such as bears, wild boars, wolves and beavers.

436 Today, habitat loss is happening at a terrifying rate, especially for tropical forests. These forests are 'hot spots' that have the richest range of wildlife, known as biodiversity. They occur mainly in Central and South America, West Africa and Southeast Asia – and this is where most endangered animals live.

▶ Tropical forests are chopped down for their valuable hardwoods such as teak and mahogany. What remains is burnt and the land cleared for crops.

437 The muriquis or woolly spider monkeys of Brazil are critically endangered. Trees in their tropical forests have been chopped down for logs and the timber trade. Then the land is cleared for farm animals and crops. The monkeys, along with thousands of other forest species, have fewer places to live.

438 In Borneo, animals from pygmy elephants to orang-utans are under threat as their forests are cleared for oil palm trees and other crops. Oil palm plantations are one of the main reasons for habitat loss across the tropics. The vegetable oil from the fleshy fruits is used for cooking, to make margarine and prepared meals, and for a vehicle fuel known as biodiesel.

191

Too many people

439 Many animals no longer live in their natural habitats because people now live there. The number of people in the world increases by about 150 every minute. They need houses, land for farms, shops, schools, factories and roads. More people means less places for wildlife.

440 Animals living in lakes, rivers, marshes and swamps are some of the most endangered. Their habitats are drained and cleared for towns, ports and waterside holiday centres. Tourist areas along rivers and coastlines endanger all kinds of animals.

▼ Across the world, cities spread into nearby natural habitats, such as this shanty town in Colombia, South America.

QUIZ

Can you name the major threats these animals face?
1. Mediterranean monk seal
2. Red panda
3. Black-necked crane
4. Golden bamboo lemur

Answers:
1. Spread of holiday areas along the Mediterranean 2. Loss of bamboo 3. Tourists 4. Loss of trees in Madagascar due to spreading villages and farms

441 The Mediterranean monk seal has suffered greatly from the spread of tourism. Its breeding and resting areas have been taken over for holiday villages, sunbathing beaches and water sports. This seal has also been hunted by fishermen, who believe it 'steals' their fish, and affected by pollution. It is now critical, with fewer than 600 left.

▲ The shy Mediterranean monk seal is frightened by boats and divers, and tries to hide in underwater caves.

442 The black-necked crane lives in the highlands around the Himalayas in Asia. It faces several threats. One is the development of tourism in a region known as the Ladakh Valley in India. People come to gaze at the marvellous scenery and watch the wildlife, but they disturb the cranes, who are shy and less likely to breed.

▶ Black-necked cranes are sometimes poisoned by pesticide chemicals used by farmers.

443 The giant panda is a famous rare animal, and its distant cousin, the red panda, is also under threat. This tree-dwelling bamboo-eater from South and East Asia has fewer places to live, as towns and villages spread quickly. It's also hunted for its fur, especially its bushy tail, which is used to make hats and good luck wedding charms.

▶ The red panda is fully protected by law, but hunting continues for its fur.

Pollution problems

444 Pollution is a threat to all wildlife, as the wastes and chemicals we make get into the air, soil and water. Like many dangers to animals, pollution is often combined with other threats, such as habitat loss and climate change. Sometimes it is difficult to separate these dangers, since one is part of another.

▲ This Atlantic croaker fish has become blind with misty eyes, or cataracts, due to chemicals in the water.

445 Harmful chemicals spread quickly through water to affect streams, rivers, lakes and even the open ocean. Caspian seals live in the landlocked Caspian Sea, a vast lake in West Asia. Industries and factories around the lake shore pollute its waters. The seals suffer from sores and fur loss, and are less resistant to diseases.

◀ Oil spillages are a devastating form of pollution. This beaver is covered in oil, which it tries to lick from its coat. By doing so it swallows poisonous chemicals that may kill it.

446

The largest amphibians in the world are Chinese and Japanese giant salamanders. They are in danger from pollution of their cool, fast-flowing, highland streams. There are few factories there, but the clouds and rains carry polluting chemicals from the smoke and fumes of factory chimneys far away.

▼ The baiji's home in the Yangtze River has become a dangerous, polluted place. The last sighting of one of these dolphins was in 2004.

POLLUTION HAZARDS

Next time you are in the park or countryside, look out for types of pollution. Find out how they could harm animals, and how we can reduce them. Look for examples such as:

Litter in ponds • Plastic bags in bushes and hedges • Pools of oil or fuel from vehicles • Broken glass • Pipes carrying poisonous liquids into ditches, streams or rivers • Metal wire, plastic tags and similar objects

447

A survey in 2006 failed to find any baijis, or Chinese river dolphins. One of the threats to this dolphin is pollution of its main river, the Yangtze or Chang Jiang, by factories along its banks, and by farm chemicals seeping into the water from fields. The pollution has harmed not only the baiji but also the fish and other animals that it eats. Further threats include hunting by people for its meat, the building of dams, drowning in fishing nets and being hit by boats.

Baiji (Chinese river dolphin)

A change in the weather

448 The whole world faces climate change, which could endanger many animal species. The weather is gradually becoming warmer because our atmosphere (the layer of air around Earth) is being altered by 'greenhouse gases'. These come mainly from burning fuels such as petrol, diesel, wood, coal and natural gas. They make the Earth trap heat from the Sun, and so the planet gets hotter.

▶ Penguins become tired after feeding in the water for several hours, and need to rest on the shore or an iceberg. Global warming means that the ice is melting and penguins' resting places are disappearing.

449 In the far north, polar bears are threatened because ice floes (big lumps of ice) are melting faster. The bears use the ice floes to hunt seals from and to rest on. There used to be plenty of floes, but now polar bears can swim for hours before finding one. Some bears even drown, exhausted in the open sea.

▶ Fewer, smaller ice floes spell terrible trouble for polar bears.

450 In the far south, penguins have trouble finding icebergs to rest on. As in the north, the icebergs melt faster due to global warming. Like the polar bears, the penguins cannot get out of the water for a rest, and because they cannot fly, they may drown.

451

Global warming is changing the seasons, which may affect huge numbers of animals. An earlier spring means that insects in Europe breed a week or two before they used to. However, migrating birds from Africa, such as pied flycatchers, swallows and swifts, might arrive too late to catch the insects for their chicks. Scientists call this 'uncoupling' of the natural links between animals and their seasonal food.

452

The huge Asian fish, the beluga sturgeon, is already endangered. It is poached for the female's eggs, which are sold as the expensive food caviar. However, as global warming continues, the sturgeon's rivers and lakes will be affected, which could push the fish to extinction even more quickly.

I DON'T BELIEVE IT!

Scientists studying 40,000 tree swallows say that the birds now lay their eggs nine days earlier than they did 40 years ago, probably as a result of global warming.

▲ Beluga sturgeons used to grow to more than 5 metres long, but most of them are now caught and killed before they reach such a great size.

Poaching and souvenirs

◀ Weight for weight, rhino horn can be worth more than gems such as rubies and pearls.

454 The main reason that rhinos are so endangered is because of poaching for their horns. The horns are carved into decorative objects such as dagger handles, or ground down to make traditional Chinese medicine. The most common use is to bring down fevers – although there is little scientific proof this works.

453 Some animals are endangered because they are hunted for trophies, souvenirs, and body parts. Poaching is the illegal killing of animals for their body parts, such as elephants for their ivory tusks.

MATCH UP

Can you match the animals with the products they are killed or captured for?

A. Tiger
B. Elephant
C. Giant clam
D. Rhino

1. Dagger handle
2. Tourist souvenir
3. Bones
4. Ivory

Answers:
A3 B4 C2 D1

455 Rhinos are not the only victims of traditional medicines.

In parts of Asia and South America, tiger bones are ground into powders for making pills, blood from sea turtles is drunk fresh, and horns of rare antelopes and gazelles are mashed into soup.

▼ This bonfire of seized elephant ivory was built in Kenya in 1989. Huge piles of tusks were burnt to try and stop the trade in ivory, but it did not succeed.

456 On holiday, some people buy souvenirs — some of which are made from endangered animals.

The souvenir trade threatens shellfish such as conches and giant clams, starfish, sea urchins, and unusual fish such as seahorses. People can buy items carved from the ivory of elephants and walruses, deer antlers and antelope horns. People should avoid all animal souvenirs (and rare plants too).

457 The trade in animal body parts and products is controlled by national and international rules.

Most countries have signed the agreement called CITES, the Convention on International Trade in Endangered Species. However, in thick jungles and remote places, it's difficult to stop poaching, while smugglers always invent new tricks to get illegal items from place to place.

▶ Buying tourist souvenirs such as dried seahorses simply supports the catching and killing of them.

199

Kill or be killed

458 **Some animals are endangered because of the threat they pose to people – at least, that is the belief.** Big, powerful predators are seen as dangerous to people, pets and farm animals. The risk of possible attack leads to persecution and revenge killing of the animal species. Hunters become the hunted.

459 **In Central and South America, the jaguar, a spotted big cat, is often killed because of the risk that it might attack farm animals.** Large areas of forest are cleared for cattle grazing, and some ranchers hire professional jaguar hunters who shoot the big cats on sight. Jaguars used to be killed for another reason – their beautiful fur coats. However, trade in jaguar fur and other body parts is now illegal.

◄ In parts of South America, hunters kill small crocodiles called caimans to sell their skins and flesh, even though it's against the law.

460 **Crocodiles and alligators are shot because of the threats they pose to people and their animals.** The endangered Cuban crocodile lives in only a small region of rivers and swamps on the Caribbean island of Cuba. It is a small crocodile, about 2 to 2.5 metres long. However, it has long been hunted because of the danger of attack, as well as for its meat and skin.

▶ Great white sharks can be lured to their death by baits.

461 The great white shark is one of the most feared of all animals. People hunt and kill it just in case it attacks swimmers. This shark is now rare enough to be on the Red List of threatened species as VU, vulnerable.

I DON'T BELIEVE IT!

About 100 years ago there were probably more than 100,000 tigers. Now there are probably fewer than 5000 in the wild.

462 Tigers face many threats, especially habitat loss, poaching and being killed in case they become 'man-eaters'. As villages and farms spread, tigers have less natural prey, and they are also more likely to wander near people and farm livestock. Another major threat is being poached for their body parts, such as their bones, teeth and bile (liver fluid) to put in traditional medicines. This fate probably affects one tiger every day.

▶ Like any hungry predator, a tiger will take advantage of a weak farm animal such as a sheep.

Eaten to extinction?

463 The bushmeat trade – hunting wild animals for food – is a growing threat to many species. People have always ventured into the forest to kill wild animals to eat. However modern rifles, traps and other weapons mean that more animals can be caught, and sold at market. This growing trade in commercial bushmeat has become a huge problem.

▲ Bushmeat is sold at many local markets such as this one in West Africa. Once the animals have been skinned and cut up, it's difficult to identify if they are protected.

464 In Africa, the drill and mandrill are the world's largest monkeys, and both are in huge danger from the bushmeat trade. Killing one of these animals and selling most of its meat provides enough money to buy a week's food for a family.

▼ For thousands of years, local people have caught and eaten animals, such as this monkey, from the forests around them.

I DON'T BELIEVE IT!

The blackbuck antelope is protected in India. It was introduced to the US, and it breeds so well on ranches that numbers have to be reduced. So it's eaten in restaurants, and spare blackbucks are sent back to India to keep up the numbers.

▶ Near Lake Turkana in East Africa, villagers have caught and killed a hippo — bushmeat hunting can be very dangerous for people, too.

465 **In West Africa, the pygmy hippo is endangered due to hunting for its meat.** This small hippo lives in thick forests and travels along regular tracks to and from its feeding areas. If hunters find a track, they lie in wait for their prey. Fewer than 3000 pygmy hippos are left in the wild.

▶ In West Africa, logging vehicles leaving the forest are checked for animals captured for the bushmeat trade.

466 **Mainly in India, and through most of Southeast Asia, bushmeat hunting is affecting more animals.** The thamin, or Eld's deer, is listed as VU, vulnerable. In some places they have so little forest left that they eat farm crops. Local people kill them to stop the crop damage — and to have a meal.

467 **In South America, the Brazilian tapir's flesh is considered a delicacy, so it is a prize target for bushmeat hunters.** It is VU, vulnerable, but its cousin, the mountain tapir, is even more at risk. There are less than 2500 in the wild and better protection is needed.

Threats for pets

468 Some animals are endangered because they are caught from the wild to become pets or captives. There is a thriving illegal trade in supplying rare animals as pets, and to personal collectors and private zoos. It is not only illegal but also cruel and wasteful. Many of the animals suffer and die on the long journeys to their new homes.

▲ Exotic pets, such as this macaw, often travel in terrible conditions, cramped and dirty, with little or no food and water. They end up in cages where they often die.

▼ Criminals dig up and steal the eggs of the Komodo dragon, which fetch large sums of money in the illegal collecting trade.

469 The world's biggest lizard, the endangered Komodo dragon, has its eggs stolen from the wild by thieves. These are sold to egg collectors, reptile breeders and lizard fanciers. This is illegal, but some people cannot resist the thrill of having such a rare egg, even if they must keep it secret.

470 Colourful, clever birds such as parrots and macaws are sometimes caught for the caged bird trade, rather than being bred in captivity. Rare species such as the hyacinth macaw, the biggest of all the parrots, and the green-winged macaw, are taken from the wild. It is against the law, but bird collectors pay huge amounts for them.

◄ This tilapia cichlid fish has a been caught from the wild and placed in an aquarium. It has a burn mark on its back from resting too near to the aquarium lights.

471 Various tropical fish are caught from rivers and lakes for the aquarium trade. Some of the rarest are the tilapia cichlid fishes of the African Rift Valley lakes. Responsible aquarium suppliers and respected pet stores know about threatened species and do not accept those caught in the wild.

472 The world's biggest frog, the Goliath frog of Africa, is taken from the wild and sold to amphibian fanciers and private collectors. Its head and body are 30 centimetres long, and it can leap 6 metres in one jump. Being so large, this frog is also a good catch for the bushmeat trade.

► In West Africa, Goliath frogs — classed as endangered, EN — are caught in nets or traps. Their numbers are thought to have halved in the past 20 years.

Island problems

473 Many threatened animals live on islands. Here, the creatures and plants have lived together for many years. They have changed, or evolved, to become specialized to their unique habitat. The small size of many islands means less animals, and the unique habitat is easily upset when people arrive.

Mangrove finch

▲ Each type of Galapagos Island finch, including this mangrove finch, has evolved a beak shape suited to eating certain kinds of food.

474 The mangrove finch, which lives on the Galapagos Islands in the Pacific Ocean, is critically endangered. It is one of Darwin's finches – the birds that helped English naturalist Charles Darwin (1809–1882) work out his theory of evolution, which is so important to science.

475 Also on the Galapagos, giant tortoises are under threat, partly due to a common island problem – introduced species. People have taken many animals to islands, such as cats, rats, rabbits and dogs. These new arrivals destroy the natural habitat, prey on some local species, and compete for food and shelter.

▶ 'Lonesome George' is the last of his kind – a Pinta Island giant Galapagos tortoise. When he dies, the species will no longer exist.

On the island of Cuba, the rare, shrew-like Cuban solenodon or almiqui, was thought to be extinct. One was caught alive in 2003. Named Alejandrito, he became a celebrity, was studied for two days, and released unharmed.

476 The island of Madagascar has amazing and unique wildlife, but much of it is in danger. Lemurs, such as the ring-tailed lemur, are found nowhere else in the wild. However, many Madagascan species are threatened by a mixture of habitat loss, hunting for food, capture for the illegal pet trade, and the problem of introduced species.

◀ Ring-tailed lemurs are popular in wildlife parks and zoos, but are becoming rarer on their island home of Madagascar.

477 On islands, not just exciting species such as giant tortoises and colourful birds are threatened. There are less glamorous species, such as the partula snails of the South Pacific islands. They were eaten by a predatory snail called Euglandina, which was introduced to provide food for local people.

478 There have been more than 700 known animal extinctions in the last 400 years — and about half of these were on islands. In the Hawaiian islands alone about 25 kinds of birds, 70 types of snails, 80 kinds of insects and more than 100 plants have disappeared in the past 200 years.

▶ Some species of partula snails now survive only in zoos or science laboratories.

Stop the slaughter

479 For more than 50 years there has been a growing awareness of endangered animals and how we can save them. 'Headline' species such as pandas, whales, tigers and gorillas grab the interest of people and help to raise money for conservation. This conservation work can then protect natural habitats and so save many other species as well.

▲ The Born Free Foundation is an international wildlife charity working around the world to protect threatened species in the wild.

480 In the 1960s, the giant panda of China became famous as the symbol of the World Wildlife Fund, WWF (now World Wide Fund for Nature). Huge conservation efforts mean the giant panda is now off the critical list, with some 2000 in the wild, although it is still listed as EN, endangered.

◄ Pandas eat almost nothing but particular kinds of bamboo, so they rely heavily on their specialized habitat.

I DON'T BELIEVE IT!

The giant panda was chosen as a symbol of conservation partly because of its black-and-white colours. These make its image easier to photocopy without the need for any colours.

481 In the 1970s, people started to protest against the commercial hunting of great whales, which was threatening many whale species. 'Save the Whale' campaigns and marches became popular. Eventually in 1980 there was a world ban on the mass hunting of large whales.

482 In the 1980s, there were many anti-fur campaigns, to stop the killing of wild cats and other animals for their fur coats. This helped to reduce one of the threats to many beautiful cat species, not only big cats, but also medium and small species such as the ocelot and margay. Sadly, fur is becoming a popular fashion item once more.

483 In the 1990s, the terrible crisis facing the tiger became clear. Save the Tiger Fund was founded in 1995 to fight the many dangers facing the biggest of big cats. However, it is too late for some varieties, or subspecies, of tiger. The Balinese tiger from the island of Bali became extinct in the 1930s, and the Javan tiger followed in the 1980s.

▶ Great whales, such as these blue whales, are now fairly safe from mass slaughter. However, they breed very slowly and their numbers will take many years to start rising again.

A place to live

484 **The main way to save threatened animals is to stop or reverse the process of habitat loss, and give them a place to live.** In a handful of cases, breeding endangered species in zoos and small parks can help, but in the end, animals need their natural habitats – not only for themselves, but for many other kinds of animals and plants living in their habitat.

▲ Bison were just saved from extinction and now roam freely in Yellowstone, Wood Buffalo and other North American parks.

▼ The Great Barrier Reef Marine Park has gradually been extended over the years, with limited tourism in some areas and complete protection in others.

485 **Natural places are preserved by setting aside large areas as national parks, nature reserves and wildlife sanctuaries.** In 1872, Yellowstone National Park in the USA became the world's first national park. As in other protected areas, there are laws preventing people from damaging the animals, plants or habitat. Yellowstone's animals include the American bison or 'buffalo', which used to roam the prairies in millions. It almost became extinct in the 1880s but was just saved.

486 Some of the most important and precious wild areas are given the title of World Heritage Site. In Ethiopia, East Africa, the Simien National Park is home to extremely rare animals such as the gelada baboon, the Ethiopian wolf (Simien fox or jackal), and a type of wild goat called the Walia ibex, of which there are only 500 left.

▲ The 500 surviving Ethiopian wolves are found in only a few areas, such as the Bale Mountains and Simien National Park in Ethiopia.

487 One of the world's biggest protected ocean areas is Australia's Great Barrier Reef Marine Park, home to amazing animals from tiny coral creatures to huge sharks. In 2006 the US set up the even bigger NorthWest Hawaiian Island National Monument. This reserve is home to more than 7000 animal species including the threatened Hawaiian monk seal, green turtle and Laysan albatross.

QUIZ

Where would you find these rare animals?

1. Ethiopian wolf
2. American bison
3. Hawaiian monk seal
4. Green turtle

Answers:
1. Simien National Park, Ethiopia 2. Yellowstone National Park, USA 3. NorthWest Hawaiian Island National Monument 4. Great Barrier Reef, Australia

Captive breeding

488 Zoos, wildlife parks and breeding centres may play an important role in saving animals. Some animals are kept and encouraged to breed and build up their numbers, hopefully for release back into the wild. This method needs expert knowledge about the species, so the zoo keepers can look after the animals well. However, it can only be used in selected cases.

489 Not only big exciting animals are bred in captivity – one of the smallest is the Chatham Island black robin. By the early 1980s, only five remained, with just one female, 'Old Blue'. Careful captive breeding involved taking away her first batch of eggs, so she would lay a second clutch, while keepers cared for the first batch so they hatched. There are now more than 250 black robins.

▼ When rare animals such as the giant panda are reared in captivity, scientists can learn much about them.

◄ Pere David's deer have been released back into their home area of China.

I DON'T BELIEVE IT!

In 1986, there were only about 50 black-footed ferrets left, all in Wyoming, USA. After 20 years of captive breeding and release, there are now more than 600 in the wild.

490 For many years, Pere David's deer lived only in reserves owned by the emperors of China. Gradually the deer disappeared – many were eaten. However, a few were taken to Woburn animal park in the UK, where they bred. In the 1980s, some Pere David's deer were released back into the wild in China, where they are still CR, critically endangered.

491 The critically endangered Grand Cayman Blue Iguana was down to fewer than 15 lizards. Since 1996, captive-bred lizards have been released into protected areas on the island of Grand Cayman, and more reserves and releases are planned.

▼ Blue Iguanas are tagged so they can be closely monitored in their protected areas.

▼ Tigers breed well in some zoos, but release into the wild is virtually impossible. Captive tigers lose their instinct to kill, so may starve to death.

492 There are many problems when releasing captive-bred animals back into the wild, especially for apes such as orang-utans. Young apes learn from their parents about how to find food and avoid danger. If they are brought up in captivity they may need to be taught by people how to become wild again.

213

Conservation ups and downs

493 Many endangered animals face a variety of threats, so helping them needs a variety of actions, all organized into a conservation programme. For example, it is little use providinga wildlife park for a rare bird if the park is overrun with rats that will eat the bird's eggs.

▶ The Arabian oryx seemed to be recovering its numbers, but these are falling again.

494 By 1972 the last wild Arabian oryx, a gazelle from the Middle East, had been killed. However, some oryx had been captured and bred, especially in Phoenix Zoo, USA. A reserve was set up in Oman in the Middle East and 10 captive-bred oryx were released there in 1981. Their numbers rose. However in 2007, Oman reduced the reserve's size. Oryx numbers have since fallen from over 400 to less than 70.

MAKE A CONDOR PUPPET!

You will need:
Old sock   Paints and paintbrush

A Californian condor chick takes food from its parent. So conservation workers 'trick the chick' by making parent look-alike puppets. Paint an old sock with the colours shown to make a pretend condor head. Would you take food from it?

▶ Pygmy hogs are about 30 centimetres tall and weigh just 10 kilograms. They were once widespread along the southern foothills of the Himalaya Mountains, in marshes and swamps with tall grasses.

495 The Californian condor is a huge bird of prey from southwest North America. Its numbers fell over many years due to habitat loss, poaching, poisoning from eating animals killed by lead shot from guns or pesticide chemicals, and even crashing into power lines. In 1987, all 22 known condors were captured for breeding at Los Angeles Zoo and San Diego Wild Animal Park. Gradually numbers increased. By the mid 2000s there were more than 250 birds, including more than 100 back in the wild.

496 The pygmy hog of the Indian region is CR, critically endangered. There are probably less than 200 left, mainly due to loss of their natural habitat for farming, and also being killed for food. One of their last areas is the Manas Tiger Reserve in the Assam region. In 1995, the Pygmy Hog Conservation Programme was founded to help this unusual type of pig to survive.

◀ Californian condors are big enough to carry radio tracking devices, so scientists can study how far they fly, and where they feed and nest.

Future help

▼ Whale-watching not only helps people to appreciate the wonders of these great animals, but also how important it is to save all natural places and their wildlife.

497 **Saving threatened animals is not just for wildlife organizations and governments — everyone can help.** You could volunteer for a conservation group, or set up a wildlife club in your school or neighbourhood. You might raise awareness by telling family and friends about threatened species, or have a 'rare animals' birthday party.

498 **Local zoos and wildlife parks often have lots of information about endangered animals and their conservation.** You can visit, write or email them, to ask if they are involved in conservation. Find out how zoos share information about their rare animals, so suitable individuals can be brought together for breeding. Wildlife conservation organizations often offer animal adoptions so you can sponsor a rare animal, maybe as a birthday present or a gift.

499 **Saving threatened animals cannot be done without saving their habitats — and taking into account people.** The people who live in the same area as a rare species may be very poor and very hungry. They see lots of time and money being spent on the endangered animal, but nothing for themselves.

500 Countries and governments must take into account their people, animals, plants and habitats, for a long-term and sustainable result. For example, wildlife can help to raise money by encouraging environmentally responsible tourism. This is when people pay to see rare creatures, such as gorillas, whales and tigers, under careful, monitored conditions. Then the money is used for local conservation that helps people as well as wildlife. Only in this way can people and endangered animals live together for the future.

I DON'T BELIEVE IT!

In 2005, a new kind of monkey, the highland mangabey, was discovered in Africa. At the same time it became one of the rarest and most threatened of all animal species.

▶ A close-up view of a tiger can encourage tourists to support campaigns to save these beautiful animals, and thereby protect large areas of their habitat for other creatures and plants.

Index

Index

Index

Acknowledgements

The publishers would like to thank the following sources for the use of their photographs:

t = top, b = bottom, l = left, r = right

Page 11 DK Limited; 13(t) Reuters; 27(t) Jaroslaw Grudzinski; 137(c) F.H. Idzerda; 143(cl) RGBKew; 194(b) Newman & Associates/Oxford Scientific; 186(t) Save the Rhino International

Alamy 29 sciencephotos; 145(br) John Glover; 146 Mary Evans Picture Library; 169(c) Picture Press; 172(t) Photos 12

Corbis 8 Annie Griffiths Belt; 10 Layne Kennedy; 20 Michael Amendolia; 33 Mike Nelson; 34 Martin Schutt; 35(t) Paul A. Souders; 36 Ted Soqui; 37(t) Reuters; 38 Michael S. Yamashita; 40 Bill Varie; 44 Ladislav Janicek/Zefa; 45(t) Louie Psihoyos; 47(c) Bettmann; 48(b) Louie Psihoyos; 141(t) Jonathan Blair; 143(br); 165(t) Alex Hofford, (b) Patricia Fogden; 169(b) Martin Harvey; 182(b) Martin Harvey/Gallo Images; 190 Frans Lanting; 192 Fernando Bengaechea/Beateworks; 194(t) Karen Kasmauski; 195(br) George Steinmetz; 196(t) momatiuk-Eastcott; 199 Owen Franken; 201(b) Keren Su; 203(t) Jeffrey L Rofman; 210(b) Theo Allots; 211 Martin Harvey; 216 Natalie Fobes; 217 Theo Allots

Fotolia.com 137(cr) Sumatran tiger Vladimir Wrangel, (br) Malayan tiger Kitch Bain, (br) Indochinese tiger Judy Whitton; 140(bl) clearviewstock; 145(c); 164(t) sisu; 167(c) Jefery

FLPA 30 Martin B Withers; 144 Gerard Lacz; 172(b) Simon Littlejohn/Minden Pictures; 176 Frans Lanting; 184 Winfried Wisniewski; 193 Panda Photo; 204(b) Tui De Roy/Minden Pictures; 205(t) Linda Lewis; 206 David Hosking; 209 Flip Nicklin/Minden Pictures; 210(t) David Hosking; 212 Katherine Feng/Globio/Minden Pictures; 213(b) John F. Binns, www.IRCF.org; 214 Philip Perry; 215 Yva Momatiuk & John Eastcott/Minden Pictures

NHPA 159(b) Bruce Beehler; 167(t) Photoshot; 182(t) Jonathan & Angela Scott; 195(t) Mark Carwardine; 198(b) Jonathan & Angela Scott; 203(b) Martin Harvey; 204(t) Martin Wendler

Dreamstime.com 137(tr) South China tiger Trix1428; 160(c) Photoinjection; 167(b) Naluphoto

Getty 156(b) National Geographic; 173(t) AFP; 183 Art Wolfe; 202(b) Karen Kasmauski; 213(t) National Geographic

naturepl.com 158–159 Eric Baccega; 168 Andrew Harrington; 200 Luiz Claudio Marigo; 205(b) Andrew Murray

photolibrary.com 202(t) Nick Gordon; 140(c) Paul Nevin; 141(br) Stouffer Productions; 157 Howard Rice; 170–171 Purestock

Rex features 45(b) Sipa Press; 147 Icon/Everett

Science Photo Library 13(b) Sinclair Stammers; 23 Alan Sirulnikoff; 31 Sheila Terry; 35(b) NASA/GSFC/METI/ERSDAC/JAROS; 39(t) Mauro Fermariello; 48(t) Pascal Goetgheluck; 134–135 Richard Bizley; 172(b) Philippe Psaila

TopFoto 156(t) Artmedia/HIP; 160(b) The Granger Collection; 161(t) The Granger Collection, (b) Topham Picturepoint

All other photographs are from: Corel, digitalSTOCK, digitalvision, Fotolia.com, ImageState, iStockphoto.com, John Foxx, PhotoAlto, PhotoDisc, PhotoEssentials, PhotoPro, Stockbyte

Every effort has been made to acknowledge the source and copyright holder of each picture. Miles Kelly Publishing apologises for any unintentional errors or omissions.

All artworks from the Miles Kelly Artwork Bank